T0199088

TRANSFORMATION

TRANSFORMATION
Never Beyond Hope

David Goad

WESTBOW
PRESS®
A DIVISION OF THOMAS NELSON
& ZONDERVAN

Copyright © 2019 David Goad.

All rights reserved. No part of this book may be used or reproduced by
any means, graphic, electronic, or mechanical, including photocopying,
recording, taping or by any information storage retrieval system
without the written permission of the author except in the case of
brief quotations embodied in critical articles and reviews.

WestBow Press books may be ordered through booksellers or by contacting:

WestBow Press
A Division of Thomas Nelson & Zondervan
1663 Liberty Drive
Bloomington, IN 47403
www.westbowpress.com
1 (866) 928-1240

Because of the dynamic nature of the Internet, any web addresses or
links contained in this book may have changed since publication and
may no longer be valid. The views expressed in this work are solely those
of the author and do not necessarily reflect the views of the publisher,
and the publisher hereby disclaims any responsibility for them.

Any people depicted in stock imagery provided by Getty Images are
models, and such images are being used for illustrative purposes only.
Certain stock imagery © Getty Images.

THE HOLY BIBLE, NEW INTERNATIONAL VERSION®,
NIV® Copyright © 1973, 1978, 1984, 2011 by Biblica, Inc.®
Used by permission. All rights reserved worldwide.

Scripture taken from the New King James Version®. Copyright ©
1982 by Thomas Nelson. Used by permission. All rights reserved.

ISBN: 978-1-9736-6104-7 (sc)
ISBN: 978-1-9736-6105-4 (hc)
ISBN: 978-1-9736-6103-0 (e)

Library of Congress Control Number: 2019904974

Print information available on the last page.

WestBow Press rev. date: 05/09/2019

This book is dedicated to Darlene, who believed in me.

Speaking as a reader, David Goad has brilliantly chronicled his dark journey from a life of drinking, carousing and away from his Lord to become a man of faith, pastoring his own church.

Carroll C. Martin – Author
"Ashes Upon the Snow"

CHAPTER 1

DEATH COMES CALLING

*I*t was New Year's Eve, around eight o'clock. People were just beginning a long night of celebration. As was a salesman for a western-wear company, I had been traveling all week for work. Promising my wife to be home early that night, as my mother was coming from out of town, to visit a few days.

I had promised to home by four at least, but stopping off at my mistress' apartment first to have just one drink with her, it did not happen. Instead, we had several drinks to celebrate the new year, time got away. When I checked my watch, I knew I would have trouble when I got home. I did not expect what was waiting for me behind the front door when I arrived though.

As I entered that door, the first thing I saw was my revolver aimed at my face, cocked with my wife's finger on the trigger. Donna was a furious wife, not in her right mind at this moment. The crazy-wild look in her eyes told me I was in real trouble. She held the gun pointed at my head. She was so close to me, there was no way she could miss if she pulled on that trigger. There was no shaking, no questions, just that pistol barrel. It looked much larger than it was I'm sure. As I looked into that barrel, she said, "I'm going to kill you, and then kill myself"! Somehow, I believed, I was the only one scheduled to die that day.

A thought flashed in my mind telling me to get my hand between the hammer and the firing pin, to grab the body of the gun. As fast as the thought came into my mind, I reached, grabbing the pistol with my hand, trying to get between the hammer with its firing pin and the cylinder holding the bullet.

Donna pulled the trigger… Silence!!

The firing pin came down on the very edge of the skin between my thumb and forefinger. It had penetrated the skin but not deep enough for the firing pin to reach the bullet that would have caused it to fire. When Donna pulled the trigger, the gun had been pointed directly at my heart.

Now over the gun barrel, were the eyes of a wild person. Realizing the gun had not gone off, she screamed like a banshee. With pure fury and hate, she let go of the gun. Instead, she attacked my eyes with both hands, formed into claws. Only reflexes caused my head to turn as those claws scraped just below my left eye and down that side of my face and neck. Bleeding, I shook my head, as realization told me that my battle with death was over for now. The revolver was now in my hands, but the clawing to my face and neck had been enough for me to need medical attention.

My Mom had come to town for a visit, but when she had come to our house, she quickly sized things up, seeing an incredibly angry woman. Knowing there would be trouble when I got home, she went to friends to wait, leaving word for me to call or come over when I could. Not dreaming of the violence or death, my wife had in mind for me.

This was only the beginning of a long ordeal of living with a person having two agendas, one loving me, the other wanting me dead. It is not that my wife did not have a good reason to hate me. Even that night I had been to my mistress's house before I came home.

Donna could not prove it, but she knew something was happening. That is one of the pitfalls of an affair. The person having an affair may think they are getting away with something, but the person that is living with one knows in their heart that something is not right, that small things have changed in the marriage.

More about that later, this is how it all started.

CHAPTER 2

THE PREDATOR

*O*h, they did not know he was a despicable man who sought an innocent child to have as his sexual plaything. Mother and Dad became close friends with this man and his family. Our family would go to his home so the parents could play cards. He was a highly respected leader in town, a man of authority, who has since passed on to his reward, whatever that is. My family trusted him. I imagine my father at least thought of the position the man had as a stepping stone to Dad being able to gain trust through their relationship with local bankers and businessmen. We kids would watch TV, read books, or play together.

Somehow this man singled me out. I do not know how it started or how he got me there. He may have picked me up from school since my family trusted him. I remember being at his house more than once. When he got me to his home, he exposed himself and molested me many times. I was young, five to seven years old. I trembled inside because he was a man of authority. A principal with such high standing, a churchman, a well thought of community leader, but he was molesting this young boy. I do not know if there were others. I tried to stay away from him as much as possible.

Somehow, he would get permission to take me home so he could have me alone. Where were my older brothers? My parents? My protectors? Why didn't someone stop him? Pedophiles are very slick in manipulating private time and isolating kids they choose.

In later years as a teenager, my Dad went to prison. With the help from the Red Cross, my oldest brother, Jim, came home from the military in England to help my Mother, my sister, Lynda and myself. Another brother, Jerry, was already fighting for our country and his life, in Vietnam. Jim came home to help us so now he became the man of the family, unfair to him as it was. Mother was close to having a nervous breakdown so Jim and I went to Houston where he could find work to care for the family. We were to go there, get a job, a paycheck, an apartment so Mother and sister could join us. We would get out of the small-town Dad had gone to prison from, having a fresh start.

When Jim and I got to Houston the first night, we stayed in a place called the Clay Hotel downtown. It was a rough area, a real dive, but we did not have much money. We had my car and a few things we could pawn to get by with until we found work. A sewing machine, a sword, and other small items we could carry with us.

We had two single beds in one room. Jim bought us both a cigar that night to celebrate the two brothers being together again. I thought I was a big stud, up there smoking a cigar with my big brother, until I started turning green from the strength of the cigar.

That night someone broke into my car stealing everything we

had, so all our pawn goods had disappeared. Our money source was gone, so were our chances of survival. Jim called Mother, she arranged for us to stay with old family friends for several days while we got on our feet.

I thought my past had caught up with me! I did not know whether to be mad or scared, a little of both.

I just knew I did not want to go, but we had no other choice. To not go I would have to tell my brother what had happened to me in my early years. We were to stay at the home of the man who had molested me those many times as a small boy!

When we got to his home, he acted as if nothing had ever happened between us. His kids were grown, and I was a sixteen-year-old teenager myself. I felt like trash while there, like I was the guilty one. I was not about to be left alone with this man ever again. I wanted to confront him, but who would believe me?

Thankfully, it did not take my brother much time with his military background to find a job. We could get out of this humiliating situation. They loaned us money to get started. I suspected he wanted me gone as much as I wanted to be gone. It was a sick, challenging time in my life. However, it helped mold me into the man I became.

The pedophile had moved and was now a man of importance in Houston. He managed a center for people with special needs. I have often wondered if it was so he could molest young boys who could not or would not report him, out of fear.

It amazes me trusted family friends or relatives are molesting how many young men and women every day. I have worked with many people over the years who have had to deal with this evil. Some overcome it, but many are scarred for life. Turning to self-medication through drugs, alcohol, sex or a life of low self-esteem and emotional difficulties. Meanwhile, the molester gets away with it by threats or guilt of the molested, innocent child. We keep quiet as victims for fear no one will believe us anyway. We are at fault, aren't we?

I lived with and fought depression for many years due to the hidden secret I carried deep in my heart and mind. Living with the guilt and fear that somehow my past would cause me to turn into a pedophile too. Praise God that is not the case with me, but some become a second generation of what has happened to them, they do to others. Some even commit suicide, with no one ever knowing the why of it. Leaving family and friends to wonder what went wrong. Or was it their fault somehow? The answer is no. It is the fault of the pedophile that molested them.

At a church event years later, I would release it to God rather than continue carrying the guilt and fear myself any longer. God helped me to realize it was not my fault. I had not done it; it was done to me. Forgiving the molester was not as easy, but I gained the freedom of mind to not let his sickness control my life.

It took years to get over the low self-esteem created, thinking I was filthy, or something was wrong with me. In time I came to understand that Jesus loves us as we are, no matter where we have been.

CHAPTER 3

LIVING WITH A CONMAN

*D*ad was a habitual conman. Crooked deals were a regular part of his life. Dad was known as a man that would give the shirt off his back if you needed it. He just did not understand it was not ok for him to go steal another shirt for himself. Dad could usually talk his way out of legal troubles then move us to a new area, often in the middle of the night, and start the same things again. Older people were his favorite targets as they are more trusting, so he could ingratiate himself with them then use that trust to cheat money out of them.

At the same time, he was having affairs with young women, once bringing a much younger woman home to live with us, under the pretense that she had no place to go and needed help. After living with us a little while, she took my brother and me to the park. While sitting on the swings, she told us that Mom was dying of cancer, but did not want anybody to know so we had to stay quiet about it.

We thought she was our friend, being young and gullible.

The young woman even cried as she told us, the tears were so convincing, that we believed her. What she or Dad had planned to do about Mom, has haunted me in my older age. Were they planning to take her life somehow then say she died of cancer? Were they planning to run away, telling us she had died? No one will ever know. Mother and Dad finally had a massive fight over the situation with the young woman being gone afterward, without an explanation to us.

Another of his scams included another woman. He had become Sunday School director in a small church, all the while sleeping with the choir director's young wife.

A local businessman that Dad had cheated found out about the affair. The businessman told Mom where and when to find Dad, with the other woman, in another town. Since both my older brothers were away in the military, it fell to me to escort Mom to the place.

We found the old hotel where Dad and the woman were to be. We even knew the room number they were supposed to be in. Mom and I went down a very long and dimly lit hall to the room. Mom was so scared she could not do knock on the door once we got there, she asked me to knock.

I was a teenager myself and scared but rapped my knuckles on the door. Nobody answered so I did it again. Harder this time! We could hear someone coming to the door, we had no idea who it would be until the door opened to Mom and me.

With few clothes on, our family friend was standing in front of us. As she realized who we were, shock then fears, registered on her face. I looked past her to movement at the back of the room. My Dad was standing there, zipping up his pants. His first words were, "Son, this isn't what it looks like!" Mom could not say anything but the woman's name. After all these years later, I can still hear the pain and agony in my Mothers voice that day.

As the first shock wore off, Mom grabbed me and ran from the hotel.

The very next day as I was driving to school, about to turn a corner, Dad met me. He stopped, rolled down his window to talk. I guess he was going to explain the events of the day before. Instead, it turned to me again to tell him the law was after him and that he should give himself up. Dad went to the sheriff's office to talk his way out of this case too, as he had done so many times before. Dad was arrested this time, for yet another matter of trying to cheat an old couple out of money by taking in their expensive piece of antique furniture to repair. Then he sold it to another customer or two.

This time his luck had run out though, Dad went to prison for three years. He served eighteen months with eighteen months' parole. During the prison time, plans were made. As soon as he was out on parole, those plans were put into action.

He cheated the people who had hired him out of prison. He left the company van at a gas station and disappeared with company funds! The last we heard of him for more than twenty years, the FBI came to Mother's door looking for him. He had stolen a truckload of new tractors from another boss' company and disappeared into the wind. The tractors were never found.

CHAPTER 4

MARRIAGES ONE AND TWO

At seventeen, I had married my high school sweetheart. We were married seven years, with the happy result of a son being born, David. We called him Davey until he got old enough, he chose Dave instead so we would not be confused when we were together. After the seven years and a messy divorce, I started a long procession of failed marriages.

The second marriage coming just two years later to Donna, who had issues I was unaware of. Oh, I knew she had some low self-esteem problems, but I figured with my incredibly positive attitude, I could get her balanced out soon. Little did I know that it did not work that way. After eleven years of marriage, I would be the one changed. But I get ahead of myself.

She had a boyfriend when we met. He would not give her up without a fight he said. I did not know that he meant literally. I was managing a department store at the time. I was at the front cash register when he walked in, he introduced himself by his nickname. He asked politely if he could talk to me privately. My first mistake was saying okay. We walked toward the back of the store where my office was. As we walked down the aisle, he quietly told me that she was his girlfriend and I was not going to take her from him, one way or another he would stop me. Along with the statement he took his hand out of his fatigue jacket to show me the pistol he held. I assumed he was serious about this thing then. As soon as he left, I went to the phone to call the police, telling them I had just been threatened. I understood that this was serious when a detective showed up soon to talk with me. When he learned the name of the man, the detective's whole attitude changed. My new friend was known to the police as a dangerous person with mental issues and drug involvement. The police had not been able to catch him committing any crimes to put him away with yet.

After several more encounters with the man, like walking out of my store after working late one night, I opened my car door to get in. Suddenly, I hear two sounds simultaneously, a loud gunshot and my car door glass shattering. I was already in the driver's seat, about to shut the door when it blew out the glass in the driver's side door. Fear rose in me with a life of its own. Somehow fight or flight took over, and flight won the battle quickly!

Next thing I knew I was speeding out of the parking lot with my car it full flight. Right to the police station, the first question was, did I see who had shot at me? The answer was no! I was too busy getting out before any more shooting could happen, to look around for who was shooting.

Officially, I was told the police could not do anything without a witness. Privately, the detective working my case came to see me with a gift. He gave me a pistol and advice. The gun was a small.38 handgun. The advice? To invite my antagonizer to my duplex apartment. At a late hour to talk this out. When he knocked on my door, to open the door and fire all but one bullet into him without warning. To be sure he was halfway inside my apartment. Even if I had to drag him inside. Then fire the final round into his head. I could not be charged because he would be an intruder into my home, shot in self-defense.

With this as a beginning, you might think a smart person would run from the relationship. I never claimed to be a smart person though. I thought I could save this innocent girl from something bad, I guess. Instead of killing my antagonist, I asked the girl to marry me.

By the time, the wedding day came around, I knew I was not in love. I just could not find the courage to hurt her. I had discovered she was delicate and afraid of her strong personality father. Not physically afraid but controlled by a fervent desire to please him or to have his approval. Those feelings were so strong that when she became pregnant, she would not admit it to herself or anyone else. You see she was a juvenile diabetic, so her Dad had instilled in her his extraordinarily fervent desire for her to never get pregnant, for her own health. The self-denial of the pregnancy even fooled her doctor, a friend of her Dads, just two weeks before we lost our 5-month-old son to a needless miscarriage.

I will never forget the empty feeling I got when the doctor came out to tell me a baby boy, I did not even know about had died in the womb. We had been with her family all day that day. Her Dad had been a medic in the Navy, he now sold medical supplies. But he never guessed that when my wife had been cramping so severely and sick that day that she might be in trouble. Instead, he treated her with home remedies until eventually, we went home. As she just kept hurting more, I took her to the hospital, but it was too late. The Father, doctor, and Donna mentioned here have since all passed away.

I should have walked away before the wedding ever happened; I know now. I thought if Donna loved me enough that I could learn to love her back, I guess.

After losing the baby, we moved away hoping things could be different and they were much better for a while. We joined a church and got involved in our small town. I was a traveling salesman, she settled into being a homemaker. There was one slight issue though.

When I was looking at places to rent, I met an amiable real estate man who told me about a beautiful apartment complex available at an extremely fair price. I asked something about the complex being so new, with such a low cost, and was told it had been built by the federal government for low-income black people in the area, but they did not have any to fill it with. Curious, I asked why not.

He explained that they did not want blacks in the community so anytime one came to ask about an apartment or house he would pull out his stack of pre-signed contracts to show them that all local properties were sold or rented already. He went on to explain that when the civil war ended the blacks were given 40 acres and a mule. Some of that property was still owned by those family descendants. But as it came up for sale, a local white person bought it. That way they were eliminating all the unwanted blacks around the area of their town. By not selling or renting to any new blacks, the community was being cleansed.

I was stunned. But being young and new to the area I kept my mouth shut. Later though, I had said something about that seeming like something the Ku Klux Klan would have done in the old days. One day our Pastor saw me at the post office and quietly explained to me that the statement I had made was not wise, one never knew who he was talking to, a random statement could cause a lot of trouble for my wife me and, especially with me being gone and her alone at home! I may be somewhat thick-headed, but even I knew that was a threat.

While living in the area, I never mentioned it again. However, in the same area, we saw firsthand a cross burning. I came across the same kind of people many years later in a different part of the United States. They were just as scary there too.

My wife and I soon moved to another town where I opened a little restaurant. We were successful for a while. But a sizeable favorite chain restaurant eventually opened down the street that soon put us out of business. We then moved back to where we had started so Donna could be around her parents more. I took a job managing a local fast food restaurant.

Always looking for a way to make some extra money, I tried the popular, at the time, worm ranching. I did not have a place to raise cattle or horses, but worm ranches were easy and did not take up much room. My friend and I tried it. We built the pens, got the cow manure from a stockyard to fill the pens with. We washed the manure to get the acid out of it, let it dry, then we ordered our herd of worms. Five thousand of the little critters. We put them in their new pens and covered them with damp newspapers so they would have something to eat. Then we set back to watch our herd grow.

A few days later we checked on the herd only to find that most of our new income-producing herd of worms were gone! Escaped into Mother earth. We reread the instructions for worm ranching to find out what we had done wrong. We adjusted and ordered replacement stock for our ranch. We had better luck this time, now had to market the new worms being born. Did you know worms are both male and female, so breeding wasn't a problem? We were now official worm ranchers with stock to sell. We even had little tiny worm lassos to rope them with and trained a few for riding when we needed to have a roundup. (okay that last part is not right, but it sounds good).

People all over the Country were buying worms to begin worm ranches too, as well as city sewage companies buying worms to feed on the sewage. With no shortage of customers, we set out to make our fortune in worm ranching. We ran our ads and soon had as many orders as we could fill. We carefully boxed up the poundage of each purchase to mail our worms and received our profit. Everything was going great, so we rented a larger space and built more pens to accommodate all the offspring we were raising.

Then the problems started happening. First, the post offices quit accepting boxes of worms. It seemed they were having two issues. One was the number of insurance claims for dead worms arriving at the customer's homes. The second was the horrendous smell of the dead worms. It seems our postal system was too slow for the worms to stay damp in the boxes. The worms bedding dried up killing our critters in the shipping process.

Not to be defeated, we began shipping by airplane. Much faster, however, it was too cold at the high altitudes and the same problems as before haunted us, until the airlines refused to carry our shipments also. We found this out after boxing an unusually large order for a city up, we drove three hours to the airport in the middle of the night, only to be told we could not ship by air any longer. We turned around and drove another three hours home, knowing that all our demanding work had been done for nothing. We did not have money if we could not ship all the worms our ranch had produced.

When we finally arrived home at five the next morning, we were so tired and heartbroken that we forgot to take the worms back out of my partner's car. We just wanted to sleep. And we did, most of the next day. With our worms sitting in his closed-up car with the sun shining on it all day. That evening I got an urgent call from my partner to get over to his house right away! I arrived and at once knew what the problem was by the horrendous odor coming from his car. Dead worms! Thousands of them! We learned why no one wanted to ship our worms anymore.

He never got all the smell out, especially when it rained the scent would come alive again. Thus, we ended our worm ranching. It was a good thing I still had a job managing the fast food place.

CHAPTER 5

THE LOST IS FOUND

*T*wenty-two years after my Dad had disappeared with that truckload of tractors, I found Dad, old and sickly. Living on the charity of a family that let him live in a little house next to their business. Someone had told me that I could get a letter one time only to his Social Security address. I wrote him a letter with all my information to find me if he wanted to. Four days later I got a phone call from him. I headed for Shreveport, Louisiana where he was.

Nervous, my third wife, Margaret, and I drove past the address just as he shuffled outside to the mailbox. He was old, worn down by time and life on the run. Cancer surgery had left him with a lower jaw that had been mostly removed on one side, what little hair was gone to gray, combed from the side of his head over the top to thinly cover it. When the wind would blow, it would stand up about eight inches high. He was much smaller than I remembered and bent from time. His shuffle could barely be called a walk. It was more like how someone would move their feet in a dance, except his dancing was a one-foot shuffle forward, then the other.

As I first laid eyes on him, without him recognizing his grown son passing by, my heart cried out for his love. The love of a son and father that I had not felt in such a long time. He shuffled back into his home as I drove around longer to accept the shadow of the man I had known. When I had recovered enough to knock on his door, he answered. We entered and were introduced to his roommate, another old guy who smoked one after another, he soon disappeared into another room. We were alone. What does one say to a father after so much time?

I do not remember much of the day except that the little house was covered in cobwebs that were yellowed from nicotine after years of two men smoking along, with many beer cans and lottery tickets.

Eventually, I moved him to my town, set him up in a small house and got to know a mostly unremorseful man. Who had run to Alaska to hide? He opened a furniture store there until the area got too hot for him again legally. His getaway was to convert all he could into cash and get back to the lower states to lose himself again. He flew to Seattle, bought a new car, loaded his few things and his money into it and drove away with intent to visit an old acquaintance from prison before finding a new hiding place. Unfortunately for him, he had all his ill-gotten money stashed in the new car when he had a bad wreck, hitting a tree. He was able to get out right of the car, just before it burst into flames. The vehicle burned up with all his money and possessions in it.

Broke and alone he made his way to the old prison mate to lick his wounds from the wreck. Somehow, he wound up in Shreveport, working for a family that felt for him and cared for him when he got cancer until I came to relieve them of the responsibility.

I asked him one time whatever happened to the truckload of tractors. His reply was short. "I don't know what you are talking about," he growled. Dad passed away from a stoke not long afterward.

CHAPTER 6

LEARNING TO PARTY

A good friend came through my town while I was running the fast food place. He said, "David, I have a better job for you if you would be interested...traveling sales for a clothing company. I feel like you would be good at it." It was something that appealed to me, but I had started the process of going to seminary. Seminary?

Yes, I had been encouraged to go to a famous seminary in Fort Worth, Texas by my Pastor. He had introduced me to the President who explained they were starting an associate degree for men without the college requirements for a full degree. Instead, I could go for two years, even though I had not gone to college, I could earn an associate degree.

With it, I could Pastor smaller to mid-sized churches. I would be the first applicant and would have the recommendation of my Pastor and the seminary President, so I was assured of being accepted.

My wife and I had even gone to Fort Worth to find housing

and work. However, when we told her family what I wanted to do we get a shock, they were totally against it. They had all the reasons lined out too. Donna listened and joined them in the discouragement of my dream. I also discovered that she would not be a good fit for a Pastors wife, as she really did not care for or about people or their needs. Therefore, I accepted the sales job, it would contribute to my decline into becoming a drunk.

The job was a good paying, traveling salesman job. One day my friend, who was now my boss said to me, "You are making your customers feel uncomfortable with you when you take them to dinner by not having a drink with them. You need to learn to drink a little beer or wine so you can be sociable with your clients." I really respected my boss, and I loved my job, so I tried a little try beer and a little wine.

That was my first step into the abyss I would find myself in later.

I discovered that the beer or alcohol made me more relaxed, it let me be more me I thought. Before long I was drinking quite a bit when I was out on the road. The next step was easier to take, that of the womanizing and the topless bars and strip clubs. I had found that some of my buyers were apt to buy more if I had shown them an 'enjoyable time' the night before.

Donna, at home, did not know about that part of my life. I could get away with it I realized. That was cool, and I had a lot of fun, I thought at the time. I did not even know I was destroying my body until many years later. My drinking also created problems in my work, so I changed from that company to a larger, very well-known clothing company. By then I had become a man that could drink and mix with the guys, be one of them. I tried to excel at everything I did. I had learned that even a person with no college, nor even a high school diploma, could excel in life with enough effort.

As my traveling sales work got more successful with larger companies, I was gone from home increasingly. Leaving Donna to be at home alone too much with her health and mental state. I came home one day to find her on the bed in the fetal position and unconscious. She was diabetic but had not been taking her shots or eating correctly. Eating lots of forbidden sweets. She was in a Ketoacidosis coma when I found her, had I gotten home much later she would not have been alive, I was told.

I was afraid she had done this on purpose. I did not think I could leave her at home alone for a week at a time anymore. Donna was a pretty and smart woman that could have done anything in life she wanted. Except she was a juvenal diabetic that fought all efforts to have a normal life. Donna battled depression and resisted any suggestions for getting help with it. We got her an automatic insulin dispenser that was carried in her pocket, but then she felt it made her a machine instead of a human.

When her doctor recommended counseling for Donna's emotional issues, her mother stepped in to stop any hope of that discussion. Her Mother took a major offense at the idea. If her daughter had mental health issues, that meant she, her Mom, must have something wrong with her too. It was true that the Mom had her own problems, but Dad was able to give her medicine to help control her issues. Dad did the thinking for the family most of the time. So, unfortunately, there would be no counseling to help Donna deal with the depression or resistance to handling her diabetes. I suspect that decision cost Donna her life later.

I changed companies again, to be closer to her family, hoping that would encourage her to be more social, to never be far away from help if needed. In all honesty, as I look back. I think I was parking Donna in a safe place while I lived my life. I was working for a major company in western wear that came with a good-sized territory.

We had regional and national marketplaces, the regional was usually held at a hotel, where we salesmen gathered with buyers. We set up our hotel rooms as showrooms by standing the bed on its side against the wall. That along with anything else we were not using would then be covered up with a cloth.

Now we opened our doors and curtains so buyers could walk down the halls looking into our showrooms to see our merchandise. We had set up portable displays to attract their attention, with many of us hiring pretty girls as models to dress in our clothes. There we did our business all day. We sold our goods to the buyers we had invited into town.

Some came only to buy the newest styles of clothing and accessories to restock their stores, but many came expecting to be entertained by we salesmen after work hours were done. Then it was time to party, while they were away from home. Often, that meant taking the buyer to dinner, and later, on to a favorite strip club to see the girls.

We worked extremely hard in the daytime, only to party just as hard at night. The hotel bar was the place to meet when we were finished with our clients for the day. The rule was, no matter how much we drank the night before, we would be up and ready to go the next morning bright and early, with a smile for the next client when they arrived.

The top Country Western music stars of that day were known as "The Outlaws." They were so popular that everyone from Texas to New York and California wanted to dress like them. People wanted to buy and wear our merchandise of boots, jeans, and accessories. We were making money hand over fist with no end in sight.

Of course, the girls wanted to hang around the western salesmen with the best products and most parties. We tried to accommodate as many as we could. We stood for the cowboys and outlaws of our day! Many of our companies sponsored the top rodeo cowboys and the top musicians or western actors. We had access to those same men and women and to the best honky tonks. We also had pockets full of cash for that liquid gold called alcohol, or drugs by some. We thought it could never end.

I had met a young girl, who became my girlfriend, I kept her on the side. She traveled with me during the week. I put her in a motel over the weekend then picked her up Monday mornings. Finally, I rented her an apartment for when we were in town. That way she could have her personal items and extra clothes somewhere that felt more permanent to her. I also promised I would leave my wife someday so we could be together forever. I would make excuses to leave home, then go to the mistress' apartment to spend time with her.

My girlfriend's apartment is where I had been on the New Year's Eve night that is the opening chapter of this book, *Death comes calling*. It is why I faced the gun when I finally got home that fateful night.

After that night with the gun, our lives changed. I would wake up during the night to hear Donna chanting. She would be beside me in the bed, sitting up on her elbow looking at me, chanting. The things she said were not what anyone would want to wake up to.

The chanting itself was a terrifying experience. Donna would be chanting to a rhythm: "I hate you; I'm going to kill you; you are a sorry son of a ..." and much worse. Immediately upon sensing my waking, the chant would change from those terrifying, hateful words to: "I love you; you are so beautiful, you are so wonderful" and other endearments.

That went on for months. I learned to wake without letting my eyes show it, without changing my breathing, listening to the chanting. One night I heard the chant turn to, "one of these days you're going to wake up with a butcher knife in your heart." When we got up that next morning, I looked under the mattress on her side of the bed. Sure enough, there was a large butcher knife. I decided she was serious.

Now I had done a lot of wrong things during that part of my life, but I did not think I wanted that knife in my heart. So, I started making plans to get away from the marriage. It did not occur to me to drop my girlfriend of four years or to become a good husband. No, that would have been too easy. I only wanted out alive, not recognizing that I was making my own mess in life and destroying others while I did it. This seems to be a common denominator for people without a spiritual compass. We only want what feels good to us at the moment. We do not consider the cost to us later or to those we effect.

I just was not ready to consider changing the fun I thought I was having at the time. It took many more lessons before I got it.

I got so good at drinking and partying that before long, I was the drunk of the group. Now, friends who were still with me would look, and I could see it in their eyes that they did not like what they saw anymore. I lost the best traveling sales jobs primarily due to my use of alcohol causing me to not pay attention to business anymore. Life had become one big party, even if I had to party alone.

Those that survived those days were the smart ones. They took care of business, entertained their buyers reasonably and stuck the money in the bank. The rest of us lived high for several years, wore our bodies out, soaked our brains in alcohol or drugs. When the bubble finally burst, we wound up broke and divorced.

In the end, I had a life in tatters, a wife, who knew I was cheating on her even if she could not catch me at it. I also had the young girlfriend in an apartment across town still, left over from better days when I had more money. She was still expecting me to leave my wife for her. By this time, she was around twenty-two, and I was closer to thirty-six. I already have said I was not a nice guy then.

I kept two homes in the same town for four years without being caught or killed outright, but not for the lack of trying through my selfishness.

My wife was out one evening, so I had taken the girlfriend to a laundromat. In taking her clothes out of my car, we missed a pair of black, silky, small panties. When I picked Donna up, and we got home, I was in a half-drunk stupor, as I was getting out of the car, I spotted something black. Picking up those shiny panties saying: "what is this?"

Instantly, I knew I was caught! Donna had seen them when I held them up. However, just then our neighbor said hi to us from his porch, in a flash that only a practiced cheat and drunk can do. I Wadded the panties in my hand, said hi to the neighbor, and excused myself, as needing to go to the restroom in a hurry. That left Donna to be polite a moment.

Rushing into the house, I tossed the panties in the heater closet as I went passed it. Then I opened my dresser drawer. By some lifesaving coincidence, laying on top was a black nylon pair of men's underwear. I threw them on the bed and made it into the restroom, just as Donna came storming through our front door demanding to know about what she had seen in my hand.

I hollered through the door that they were my undies, that I had taken them with me to the lake that day, in case I had wanted to go swimming.

With mine laying on the bed she had nowhere to go with the questions, so it was dropped. But never was it forgotten, as I soon found out, when Donna met me at the door with my gun on that fateful New Year's Eve night. Donna and I divorced eventually.

Donna died a few years later when her car crashed into a tree on her way home from work. Donna was a good woman that I surely did not do right by her.

CHAPTER 7

ONE WOMAN TOO MANY

*S*oon after the divorce from Donna was final, my mistress became my third wife. We had been together for about five years by then, we only lasted another five. The daily realities of life together were not as good as she thought it would be. Some say the age difference of sixteen years made the breakup happen. I think what starts in the wrong way, just does not end as living happily ever after.

I could not find a decent job on the road anymore, my new wife did not trust me to be a traveling salesman for some reason, so we started a business. We did well for several years. A promotional marketing company with some interest in the country music industry.

However, paybacks are tough, especially when getting divorce papers from Margaret, wife number three. It was a total blindside for me. She got the profitable part of our business while I dealt with the loss of her, what was left of our business, and the tax people that came to collect the back taxes. I had thought that those taxes had been paid. Another family member had been our bookkeeper. Later I found the tax papers in a drawer, all filled out and signed, but the checks I had signed were no longer attached. We went up for auction to pay those taxes. That was the end of our business and marriage.

Soon after the divorce and loss of our business, I also lost my continental when the repo boys showed up. I took the last of my money to buy an old ranch pickup for a hundred and fifty dollars. It was dented all over, the paint was missing in places, the bed of the truck was sitting lopsided, one side was higher than the other, with a crushed part on the tailgate. In fact, when driving down the road, anyone behind me could see that my truck looked to be going sideways. It was so out of Alignment, the shocks were out, and It had no muffler, so when I racked the pipes, it would nearly deafen anyone close to it. I got so I loved that ole' truck, as we saw lots of miles and troubles together. I even lived in it once or twice.

The cowgirls loved it when I was dressed in my triple starched jeans and a shirt so stiff it was called bulletproof, my Stetson and my pretty blond cocker spaniel dog, all dressed up too. I could just never teach her to wear a Stetson though.

While all that sounds like I was having fun, the reality is that I was living in one room of the business building, cooking on a one burner propane rig loaned to me. I would cook over the weekend enough that I could live on leftovers all week. However, that left the smell of cooking in the building all week long though.

Finally, I had to send merchandise, I had been entrusted with, back to the companies it had come from. One saleslady from our main supplier told me "I just can't respect a man that can't pull himself up by his bootstraps and carry on." Of course, it was not her that the tax man was coming the next day to carry off all the remaining inventory to an auction. After the merchandise was gone, I sold what equipment I had left and closed shop. I guess the hardest part was having to let my employees all go, including my teenage son.

After that, I just got drunk, for as long as the money lasted and then as I could get credit still at my favorite bar.

CHAPTER 8

THE BLACK PIT

*A*t one time in my journey, the self-loathing caused me to look into the black pit. I thought then, there was no way out.

One day as I dealt with the failed relationship of ten years or so, I stood in front of a wall, in my mind's eye. The wall had a huge mirror on it, the reflection I saw looking back at me began to get lumpy, saggy and out shape. Like a carnival, the house of mirrors does with the different visions of self-seen in all the various mirrors. This was just one mirror that kept changing images slowly.

There was a loud crack when the mirror suddenly began to fall into small pieces right in front of me. I was left looking at a massive hole in the wall. The hole was at least as tall and wide as I was, behind the wall was shadowy darkness with a visible brick wall showing through the darkness,

There I stood with a broken mirror at my feet. Each piece of the mirror had a small part of my reflection still in it. Most puzzling to me! As I stared at the scene before me, not sure what was happening, I leaned over the broken pieces of mirror to better see behind that hole left in the wall, to study that shadowy darkness better with the brick wall. Still further back, I heard the loud, ear-splitting crack again. The brick wall was now falling to a pile, but it fell into the blackness. As it crumbled, I could see nothing but utter darkness. I moved closer to the hole in the wall, then somehow found myself falling, falling, falling into the blackness itself.

Living in the utter emptiness of this new reality, I somehow continued to function even though in a daze, often drinking myself to oblivion. While stumbling around sometimes. A loose brick of my sanity would be found. When this happened, it was a cause to celebrate. I thought if somehow enough bricks were found they could be stacked back up so I might find a way out of the black pit.

Trying to drink myself into death or good moods, it did not matter which, thinking that the women and drinking buddies could help me find some bricks. Occasionally on a good day, I would happily announce I had found another brick. Friends thought I was crazy, and I was, for a time. Slowly the thought that I might be extremely depressed came to mind, so I drank more to cover the depression with a happy face.

It only seemed to have the ability to show itself if I was drinking heavily. We would laugh and carry on and pretend we were having an enjoyable time, but when alone I knew I was still in the black pit.

During this time, I did many things that should have ended my life. One of those times, I went to a roadside park in the hills one night with some drinking friends. As usual, we got drunk, I got into an argument with my girlfriend and decided I would walk home. The home was a good ten miles from the park we were at, but of course, I did not think of that.

As I'm walking down the road, I noticed a car coming up behind me. Figuring that it was my friends coming to find me and still being mad, I decided to hide from them. Without thinking, I just moved to get off the road, next to me was a guard rail. I grabbed the guardrail and swung over it. As I was in the swinging over, I looked down into a black void. I remember thinking this was not good.

I found myself in the air falling. After about ten feet of darkness, I hit the ground and began rolling over and over faster and faster until I hit a cactus patch. Rolling threw and over the cactus I was filled with cactus spines now too. I sensed something above me, so I reached out to stop myself. Unfortunately for me, it was a barbed wire fence that sliced my hand as I went through it too. Still rolling over and over, I finally came to a stop when I hit a tree.

With ribs injured and cactus spines embedded in my body, I lay still, thinking that if I just laid hear I might die, and my suffering would be over. Slowly reality set in that I was off the road with no help. I was laying in a pasture in the dark if I was going to get out of this mess, I was going have to move.

I carefully crawled up the hill I had just come down. I removed my shirt as it was rubbing me, increasing the cactus pain. When I got to the road, at one or two in the morning, I still had several miles to walk. I was quickly sobering up now with ribs hurting and the cactus, in me.

This time I was glad to see car lights behind me. As it began to slow down, I realized it was the friends. I gladly excepted a ride this time.

The next day at the doctor's office the barbed wire damage

done to my hand was full of trash. The doctor looked, asked how it was done, then he said to "if you are going to keep getting drunk you can clean up your own mess." He would sew it up, but I had to clean it up first myself. He gave me q-tips and iodine then told me to call the nurse when I was done. Ouch! That hurt worse than my bruised ribs.

He also would not spend his time pulling the cactus needles out of me. Instead, he showed me how to do it, sewed up the palm of my hand and sent me home. Lesson number four hundred forty-two was learned!

Other incidents that were brought on by alcohol. My family's favorite was my walking into a biker's bar one afternoon, just coming out of the sun it took a bit to be able to see.

While standing by the door this voice, from the dark, said something about my pink shirt and what kind of person wore one. First, it was not pink, it was rose-colored! I could begin to make out a man and woman sitting at the bar laughing now, she had a lot of tattoos, so I made an unflattering comment about the woman and her tattoos. The biker said to be careful what I said, as she was his 'ole lady.'

Now you would think a person with even a half a brain would know better, but I had been drinking quite a bit already, so my next comment was not well thought out. I said something close to "excuse me, thought that was your dog."

Next thing I remember she was hanging on my back while he was working hard on my front. Thank goodness, the bartender did not want any police out there, so he came out from behind the bar with a ball bat.

I somehow got a lucky blow in as my adversary's nose was bleeding, but the screaming in my ears of that woman was what really hurt me. The bartender detached her from my back, then ushered me out with a warning not to come back. He enforced it with a last tap of the ball bat.

Making my battered way to my girlfriend's apartment for sympathy, more surprise awaited me. She had no sympathy at all, instead, she poured rubbing alcohol on all my many cuts and abrasions except the now very black eye, with the admonition that if I thought I was tough, we would just see how tough I was, as she poured the rubbing alcohol on all the open wounds she could find.! It quickly sobered me up for that night.

Still, the black pit had more for me to experience before I would finally find my way out of the darkness.

CHAPTER 9

THE BOTTOM OF THE BARREL

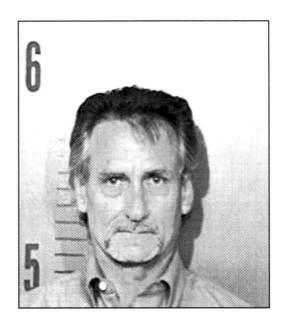

*T*he beginning of the end came on a Saturday night. I walked out of the bar at one or two o'clock. I do not know when it was. I know that I drank until the bar closed, went to my ole' truck, got in, then I remembered seeing a flat tire on the back. Sitting there a few minutes thinking I did not want to change a tire at this time of night, too drunk to realize how foolish that thinking was being. I thought I could make it home, so I did not change the tire, taking off down the highway. Made a left turn on a main street, toward my little garage apartment.

Suddenly there were flashing blue and red lights behind me. Quick thinker that I was, I decided to talk my way out of it, telling them my friend was chief of police. I got out of the truck, the officer spoke to me, he could see I was obviously drunk. Driving down the street with sparks flying out from the back of the truck will say to an officer all he needs to know.

There were broken pieces of the tire left on the rim, and scattered down the road behind me, leaving a trail of guilt. But mostly I was driving on the rim. As the officer started to question me, the first thing I said was my friend is chief of police. He said, "That's good, you can call him when I get you to the jailhouse."

"How far do you live from here," he asked. "Just a few blocks," I answered him. "That's too far. So, you got to go to jail," the Officer told me. I had never been to jail. My Dad was in prison, and I swore I would never go to jail, but there I was, about to be handcuffed and taken to jail. They cuffed me and put me in the back of his police car. He took me to jail.

When we drove around the back of the jail as I started to sober. The officer parked, got me inside and started talking to me. The next thing I knew I was standing in front of a measuring rod. They took my picture front and sideways then fingerprinted me. I went through the humiliation of all those things.

They took me to the drunk tank to lock me up with all the other drunks. The drunk tank is a grey-walled, large cell. It has a two-inch-high lip of concrete running down the sides of the cell for people to sit on. In the middle of the cell, there is a drain hole for people vomiting. It has one toilet with very little privacy. Then you have all the men there, mostly drunks or druggers, a few thieves or worse are mixed in for flavoring. They can hear you and smell your stink being sick and worse. It is not a pleasant place to be.

You can sit there all night, on the little ledge or out on the main floor. If you get up and move around, you disturb others. Disturb the wrong person, and they are going to come up fighting. So mostly you just sit. Occasionally talking to the person sitting next to you, but everyone is in the same condition you are in. Drunk or high and no one wants to talk much. No one is happy to be there.

The next morning, they came in and took us to the regular cells, locked us up in population. I swore for the first time that when that bail bondsman came, that I would never be back. But I was four more times. I was back those four more times before I took the advice of family and friends and just got out of the state.

CHAPTER 10

CALIFORNIA

*A*fter being warned by family and friends to quit drinking or get out of state, I had the decision made for me. I married Chrystal, my fourth wife, despite all that had happened between us and having been warned not to. I did anyway. Why? The answer is complicated. She accepted Jesus as her Savior and committed to changing her life. She also committed to, as she was fond of saying "I married you for a lifetime, not just a minute." Plus, she was an outdoors person, that taught me to love camping, later we got into gem and gold hunting.

Shortly after the backyard wedding, we got the call from her Dad that changed my life forever. He had prostate cancer with no more than three months to live. We got her to San Diego, California where he lived.

After a couple of weeks, it was clear he would not last long, so she needed to stay there with her family until she was finished with the saddest thing she would ever endure.

We did not have the money for me to fly back and forth so I

decided to take our 1978 blue, with custom painting, conversion van back and forth when I could. I sold or stored all our household goods, loaded the van with things to sell for gas and took off on the 1500-mile one-way journey.

I was to sleep in the back seat, so it was left empty. Inside it had a fancy roll and tuck padded ceiling, shag carpet, tinted windows, Side double doors, and rear double doors. As I was to learn later, it was a natural looking smugglers van.

The first night on the road I did not get too far because I had been drinking, got sleepy quickly. With no money for motels, I just found a likely looking side dirt trail to pull off on. Opening the side and back doors, I promptly was asleep.

Around midnight, a light in my eyes woke me, with a voice attached to it asking what I was doing there? My first thought was, I am about to be robbed, shot and left here! Then the light and voice named themselves as the sheriff's dept.

What I had thought was a pasture entry, was the rancher's driveway. The rancher and his family had come home, found the suspicious looking van parked in their drive, with all the doors open. They were afraid drug people were invading them, I guess. At any rate, they had called the sheriff.

I had to convince him I had just pulled over to sleep a while and had no intention of harming the family. He said there was a rest area just down the road a little way I could use, but these folks were tired and wanted to go home. I moved quickly, thankful that I had not been arrested for drinking again.

I would learn to bring old west things from Texas to sell in California and take stuff like seashells or shark's teeth, or anything that had been repurposed from trash in alleys to Texas to sell. This bought the gas, food, and alcohol for travel and began to do a passable business of what is called a 'picker' for antique stores.

I learned to love these trips of solitude back and forth, even started taking time to get off the freeway visiting places along my way. I loved going to Tombstone and Bisbee, Arizona when I could. My only problem was the amount of beer I consumed on some of these side trips. And the gas – alcohol had to be paid for by my picking sales along the way.

If I ran out of stuff to sell too soon, then I just pawned some personal things till my next trip, then recover them.

My only regret of these trips is when I decided to make the side run to Bisbee one day after drinking way too much and having spent my last money on said drinks. Bisbee is a long way up in the mountains above Tombstone. It was already night when I got there, so I found an empty parking lot and pulled in to sleep and to sober up. That worked fine until the next morning when I woke to an empty tank of gas and no money.

I had some success at garage sales buying in San Diego, so I set off to find an antique store. Bisbee is a small tourist town that used to be a glory hole for silver mining back in the western days. It had only one store that could be called a collectible sales store more than antique, but it would do if they were in a buying mood.

Most pickers have a regular route of stores who buy from them instead of just walking in and hoping. But I was new at this, so I just hit whoever was open. A genuinely nice lady ran this shop but did not have much money. I am quite sure she could tell I was hung over badly and really wanted to help me get on down the road.

I was not feeling well or not thinking clearly. One of the things I could get the interest in was a fly-fishing creel. A creel is the side case one carries when trout fishing to place the catch in and are an excellent item to sale. They are sought after by collectors. The lady only had thirty-two dollars, and I was desperate for gas and beer money, so I sweetened the pot with the items in the creel. There were odds and ends that I had put in the creel for storing until they were sold. I was so hung over that I really did not pay attention to what was in the creel other than I saw some stamps. I always looked for old stamps when I found old envelopes, thinking this was a mix of that type stamp, it did not seem like a big deal to include them in the sale.

She got an excellent deal that day, and I hope that she was smart enough to research all that was in the creel. I realized later that in that creel were the stamps from my Grandmothers. There were six "Jennie inverted byplane" stamps. Just one sold for 135 million dollars. They are highly sought-after stamp by collectors around the world. I had found the six stamps in an old shed at my Grandmothers house.

Six rare stamps worth several millions of dollars, traded for thirty-two dollars cash, sold by a drunk, for some gasoline and another six-pack of beer.

CHAPTER 11

UNUSUAL MEETING

*A*fter Crystals Dad passed, we stayed a while to help her Mom figure out what to do with her life next. After a while we decided to just move there, we loved the ocean, the desert, and the mountains, all within a few minutes' drives.

The issue was the cost of living was much higher there, so we both got jobs and rented a small trailer house, it is all we could afford. It was in a small trailer park, that was quiet itself, but we could hear gunshots many nights. Leaving me to wonder who was in trouble or dying that night somewhere within our hearing. On occasion, the trailer would shake or roll as an earthquake would happen somewhere. It was usually many miles from us, we would only be feeling the shockwave of the movement of the earth.

We were on the very end lot with a side street beside our fence, we could get to know neighbors after a little time. Ramon, who was a large and friendly man, who often walked from his home across the street, using our park for a shortcut to a shopping area close by. Or the little lady with the handicapped dog whose back end was in a rolling sling type contraption. The little guy had been parlayed in the hind legs from a car hitting him, but he would scamper down the street unaware that he was different. We got to know them well as they would stop to visit over our fence any time, we were outside. Of course, drinking when off work was routine, often sitting in our little yard.

I was amazed at all the green around me in southern California, with the big date or eucalyptus trees and the beautiful flowers and ice plants everywhere.

Once after a strong wind storm had come through the area. A very tall tree had to be cut down to keep it from damaging homes nearby homes. In the top of the tree was a nest of crows. Two small babies were rescued from the nest, abandoned by the parents when the cutters were working. Someone brought the two little ones to us to raise. My wife had rescued other birds and animals for people in the neighborhood before, so they thought she might be able to do something for these two. And she did, she feed them by hand until they got big enough the eat on their own. We built them a cage on the side of our house. When they were old enough, she helped them figure out they could fly, but they always came back home.

Until finally one got killed when hit by a car as it was gliding into the home. The other, named Jack, of the Jack and Jill pair, continued to stay home. He loved to steal anything shiny I might leave out on my workbench. The one day we noticed we had increased crows showing up on the highlines by our home.

They would circle in flight or land on the lines and call out, making an awful noise. Until Jake would join them. Then fly off somewhere. But Jake still came home every evening. It would start over the next morning. Until one day Jake did not come home anymore.

California was an exciting time for me, I had barely been out of Texas or Oklahoma before moving to Southern California. The climate was so nice year-round, The Palm trees and eucalyptus trees were so tall and beautiful. The flowers everywhere were so colorful. We loved going to the mountains or the ocean.

Then I discovered the dessert, I never would have thought the desert could be so beautiful. We liked to go for drives looking for gemstone locations. Or travel to old mining ghost towns to find treasures if old equipment or tailings pits, Tailing are the scrap earth left when digging for gemstones or gold and Silver. Lots of the tailings pits still had gems or Precious metals in them. By working these pits, we found lots of leftover mining treasures.

On one of these trips to explore new sites, we got stuck in sand way out in the desert. With no cell phone signal, we set up camp for the first night to enjoy the desert sounds and the brilliant stars that can only be seen best away from all city lights.

The next morning, I tried digging us out but to no success. I walked back a mile or so to a dirt road we had followed into the desert. There were vehicle tracks from heavy vehicles, so I assumed there were other campers further down that road, they should be coming back out soon. Putting a large Help with an arrow pointing to us in the middle of the road, made from the desert rock, I made my way back to our van. We spent the second-night out, but we're still not worried because we had plenty of water and food for the weekend. Those motor homes would be coming out by Sunday night.

However, the next days came and went with no help, then we heard the vehicles on the road. I started that way so I could guide our saviors back to our stuck van. As I topped a small rise, I was happy to see a procession of military trucks moving down the road. Getting closer, my joy turned to dismay as I realized they were ignoring my help sign. I started running, but by the time I got close they were gone, so was our hope of help. They had not even slowed down, just ran over my help sign.

Being caught in the desert with water running out and food gone we were in trouble. When I got back, Crystal was getting scared now. And it was too late in the day to try walking out. We spent another night in the desert. We talked about our situation. We only had a half gallon of water left. We decided that I would have to try walking out for help early the next morning before the days heat set in., we divided the water, I took our cell phone with me in case I found a signal area. We had looked the night before at where the only light we could see was and marked it on a hand made a map. I would then know which way to go at least. We knew we were miles from the paved turn off we had taken to get here but also knew that turnoff was miles from a town.

The estimate was twelve to fifteen miles from help. With lots of desert between us and hope. Crystal had twisted her ankle earlier in this trip so she could not go with me. She had to trust me to find help to rescue her from this mess we were in.

I took off at daylight. Asking God, whom I did not talk to often, for help. In the desert it is hot in the daytime, it had been up to one hundred twelve degrees the day before. It is also easy to get turned around in the desert. Between the heat and the heat waves, looking like lakes, everything starts to look alike after a while, making it easy to go the wrong way. I had taken off across the country, keeping the dirt road on my right so I could find it easily if I did not intercept it along the way.

The desert has snakes and large poisonous scorpions in it, among other things like bushes that all have spikes or thorns on them. There are also lots of holes on the desert floor to step into that will break a bone, if you are not watching constantly. I had walked a few miles before I came to a high spot and heard the ding of the cellphone telling me I had a signal. It was not a constant signal nor a strong one, but at least it was something. I called 911, but before I could give directions to our van, the signal dropped. Calling again and again, I finally got the message through that we needed help. They said they were sending a rescue team with a helicopter to find us. For me to go back to the van and wait.

I turned and started back, but after nearly stepping off into a deep arroyo that I had not come across when walking out, I realized I was lost. Wandering around in the desert in the summer is not a good way to live to a ripe old age. I needed someone to help me find the van and Crystal as she waited for my return. Trusting her life to my getting help to rescue her from that ever-present heat. Hoping I was now moving in the right direction, I started out again. Finally, the white van could be seen in the distance.

Getting close to it, I heard the helicopter circling the van. Later Crystal told me they had talked to her over a loudspeaker while hovering above her. When she knew she was going to be ok, she cried, releasing the growing fear. Help was on the way! Soon we heard the park ranger's jeep, then a dune buggy. The dune buggy backed up to our van, hooked a bungee cord to us that was a hundred feet long. One man got in our van, put it in reverse when the buggy took off at full throttle, the van was given full gas. When the buggy hit the end of the bungee cord that was now stretched out like a rubber band. The van shot out of its hole in reverse till they were clear of the soft sand we had fallen into. We were saved!

After three days and four nights in the desert with daytime temperatures well over 100 degrees, we were going home. Thus, ending our adventure, for a while at least. The dune buggy driver gave me his card, say to call him whenever we came back anytime.

Just tell him where we were going so that if we were not back out at the set time, he could come to get us.

Meanwhile, we had met a couple living across the driveway, in our trailer park, who were devoted Christians. Their grown daughter, whom they obviously loved dearly, had died a while earlier, I wanted to know how they could be so happy, and followers of Jesus after such a cruel loss. I thought if I got to know them, I could prove my theory, that all the 'Jesus' talk was the same, just so much talk. With no bases of truth.

I had forgotten my grandmother's devoted love for Christ, or I had decided she was the only exception. So, I listened to the neighbor's talk and their outward love for each other and their Jesus, waiting for when the real person of bitterness and hate would show itself. Then I could go on with my life, knowing I was right about that Christianity stuff.

Bill and Joyce Budd were the names of this couple that intrigued me. For some reason, I could not explain, I was drawn to them, but always watching for the crack in their talk to show itself. I just knew that they could not have lost the daughter, that had been the apple of their eyes, and not be bitter at the God they professed to love and follow so much. Why would a loving God, take the life of one so loved by her parents? It did not make sense to me that they would still trust God, even if He were real?

Then came the day Bill invited me into his motor home parked in the drive between our houses, to hang out. He was reading the Bible all the time; he would try to explain to me what it meant. He carried a small New Testament in his pocket and boy was it worn, as well as marked up with notes and underlined parts.

One day as we sat talking about what he was reading that day, he asked me a simple question that stopped me in my tracks. He said, "Dave, I think God is trying to say something to you, are you listening?" Well, I did not even want to listen, but later my wife and I started talking about it some. We also tried that church with her friend some more.

It seemed like every time I saw Bill; he would repeat his question to me. I doubt that it was as often as that, but it rang in my head constantly. I could tell that my Grandmother's teachings, and the example that she had set for us grandkids, had stayed with me more than I had realized. Because Bill often would read from his Bible or say things that Grandmother had taught us when we were young.

One day when Bill and I were sitting in his motorhome, we had the side door open for fresh air, and a quick getaway if things got too much for me, with his constant teaching me from that Bible. We always had an enjoyable time together at any time we got to hang out any, despite his teachings.

This day, however, Bill asked me again if God was trying to say something to me? Something was stirring inside me, so much that I needed to just get away from the question, that meant getting away from Bill too. Saying I needed to do something at home, I excused myself and started to leave.

I was on the upper step of the motorhome when in my mind started a picture like I had never seen before. As I descended the short stair steps of Bill's motorhome, the image became more evident. I rushed across the driveway, thinking I could escape the now brilliant picture of Jesus, knocking at the door of my soul. The image did not go away. I sat down in our living room to think.

I could almost hear Jesus as He looked at me with the saddest eyes I have ever seen. He had tears in His eyes, He seemed to be saying to me, it was my time. I suddenly knew beyond a dought that Jesus was telling me, "This is the last time I will knock at your soul, if you want Me, accept Me now. If not, I won't knock again."

Now I do not claim any unique insights to God, but the experience scared me in a way that is not explainable if you have not had it. The closest I can describe it was like being at the end of my life, and suddenly knowing beyond a doubt, there really is something after this life. What was I going to do about Jesus?

We each must make our own choice about what we believe. Is Jesus real? Is Satan? Heaven or Hell? We each must choose whether we believe in Jesus or not. It is not enough to believe in God, but not God's Son Jesus.

Many say they believe in God, but God says in His Bible, that we must believe that God sent his Son, Jesus, to pay the price for us to get into eternal Heaven. If we just believe in God's Son Jesus, we can enjoy life after our earthly death in Heaven forever. Now that is a big ask, and not everybody will believe, God gives us a free choice to decide for ourselves if we believe or not.

For me, I chose right then, to believe. If I am wrong, I will have been a better person in this life at least. But if I am right, I will pass from this earth into eternity with Jesus and the Father, God himself. With God's promise of life with no more pain, addictions, death, illness,' and so much more, as told in the Bible. What choice will you make?

We cannot just go through life blindly ignoring our death and what will happen at the end of it. That day, with the picture of Jesus and the conversation I felt in my mind, *transformed* me forever as I shouted aloud, "God if you are real. Heal me or kill me now, I can't go on living this way!"

My *Transformation* in life started that day, thanks to Bill Budd being faithful to his beliefs and not being afraid to share that belief. God had been talking to me, now I listened for just one second, that is all it took. One second of opening my soul, eyes, and ears, to find what I had searched for so long, an absolute peace in my life that I had never known before.

Oh, I had seen it in my grandmother and other lives, I just had not figured out that I could not manufacture it myself. All the positive attitudes, sales ability, partying, wives, business accomplishments, girlfriends, or alcohol could not find that peace, it just took the Jesus One Step. Will you take your one step toward Jesus today as you read this?

If so, take the 'Jesus One Step' to transform your life and find that love and joy that only He can give us. What is the Jesus One Step? It is simple. We take the first, one step, toward Jesus when we start our conversation with Him. Just tell Jesus you want to follow Him, even if you do not understand exactly what that means. Jesus then meets you wherever you are in your life to begin your journey in learning about who Jesus is and what is meant when in the Bible, the book of John, chapter three, verses sixteen and seventeen. Is says:

16 For God so loved the world that he gave his one and only Son, that whoever believes in him shall not perish but have eternal life. 17 For God did not send his Son into the world to condemn the world, but to save the world through him. New International Version (NIV)

You can take that one step to Jesus by saying a simple prayer: *"Dear God, I know I'm a sinner, and I ask for your forgiveness. I believe Jesus Christ is Your Son. I believe that He died for my sin and that you raised Him to life. I want to trust Him as my Savior and follow Him as Lord, from this day forward. Guide my life and help me to do your will. I pray this in the name of Jesus. Amen."* From the Billy Graham Association.

If you just said this prayer, Congratulations! You have just taken the Jesus One Step, to begin your transformation, with a new life in Christ. Contact me at davidgoadministries.com, for more information about your new journey with Jesus. We will send you free literature to help you along your journey.

CHAPTER 12

A NEW LIFE IS BORN

*T*hings began to change in our home and lives. It was not easy, but I cannot remember that it was especially hard either.

The nights, like the one, of being in a bar when the man sitting next to me decided to celebrate by shooting off his pistol, firing randomly at anything that appealed to him. I dove for cover first, then realized I was one who could stop this rampage before someone was killed.

Looking into the eyes of the person on the other side of the man shooting, who was on the floor too. Something communicated between us in the eye contact, as we both were up and grabbing the shooter, just as he turned the gun on the mirror behind the bar. Shattering it with a loud crash. As it went to the floor, so did we, with our man and his gun.

The other patron got a grip on his arm and hand, still pulling the gun's trigger, while I went around his middle. As we fought with him on the ground, the gun slipped from his hand. It was over as quickly as it had started. We held the now screaming man down until the police were called to haul the guy away, with no one hurt worse than a few bruises, and a significant case of the shakes, when it was over. The other patron and I drank a couple of free drinks and tried to laugh about our narrow escape with death. Someone had been watching over us that night, but in my new life, I did not have to put myself in the position, where it was needed to face these type things anymore.

Compared to that and other wild nights, getting sober, with the help of the new awareness of Jesus in my life was a cake walk. First, I started substituting a German made nonalcoholic beer for my usual brand of alcoholic beer. After a while, I decided we were spending so much on the German fake beer that we might as well give it up too.

We started attending a Thursday night home group of people of about ten or twelve and going to church on Sunday mornings, we began to change our way of thinking. Asking all these questions about, was God real, how Jesus and God fit together, and many others. It was overwhelming at times, if Bill had not continued to love and encourage me, I might have dropped out of this new life at times.

Then came the day that we were finishing a study in our home group. The leader asked me to decide what the next study should be that would be of interest to me.

It so happened that I had met with a Pastor in our church a few times, he had suggested meeting once a week to explore this new book he had and thought I might like.

You see, I have always been an overachiever in whatever I was doing, be it in sales or drinking. This time it was about God and telling everyone I could about this new life I had found or instead it had found me.

However, I had no experience except for my sales background. I realized much later that God was using these different men, to mold me in a way I did not understand. They were doing their best to teach me, giving me time to mature in this new life, before I could storm the world from my excitement.

At home, I was consumed by this new word, faith. With feeling God's calling me to spread the 'Good News' of Jesus' forgiving love.

We made list after list of questions a person would have about God and this new life. We read the Bible, I studied with my Pastor friend. Then one day the sky opened, and a totally new concept dropped from Heaven, through the author of the book we were studying at the time, right into my lap.

It said, "Don't just go out and start something new: "look where God is at work and join Him there." (Henry Blackaby)

That was it! All I had to do now was find that spot where God was already working, and I could be useful. I began praying for God to show me where He was already working so I could join Him in that work.

As I was reading a local Christian newspaper one day, I saw this interesting article that told about a local businessman, giving a Video about Jesus to people for free! He needed help, if anyone was interested, call him.

Deciding to call him so I could find out what this Video was about, I made the phone call that changed the rest of my life. It was a call to Bob Brown, who promptly, and rightly so, thought I was a quack.

He referred me to the regional offices for the San Diego area. When I called them, they probably thought the same, as my excitement was growing, and my marketing mind was working overtime.

We met a few days later so I could share my story with the director while learning about the video of Jesus.

The video was produced by a large international ministry. I learned there were two branches of the video project. One was the international group who had the movie in many languages to be shown in any country where volunteers would go, often with lives in danger, to show the people of the area, the film about Jesus Christ.

Then the USA branch that worked in America only with the video. The local area was managed by a volunteer, who was appointed as a leader for the city. I needed his permission to move forward if I were to volunteer to be involved with the organization.

He listened politely to my story, then gave me a Video with instructions to take it home. To view it completely, then give him a call if I was still interested.

I watched it over and over. The video was about Jesus, as written in the Gospel of Luke. It tells Jesus' life from a miraculous birth to a horrible death on a Roman cross. But goes beyond that death, to Jesus rising from the grave in three days. After being seen by many people in different circumstances! Jesus leaves instructions with His disciples then ascends back to Heaven, as is promised in the Bible. In the end, it offers the invitation to accept Jesus as our personal Savior so we can spend our life after death, with Him in Heaven forever. All its costs is our willingness to believe in His story through something called faith.

Faith is believing in something we cannot physically see, like the wind. We can see its results but not the wind itself. Well, that was not so hard for me to believe.

What I had believed a bottle of alcohol could do for me, did not work out so well. I was already happier and more at peace than I had ever been.

This Video told the story for me. It also gave the person watching it, the opportunity to accept Gods plan for their lives. I could not see any way to fail by getting involved with the Project.

As I found out, the idea was to organize churches to buy the Videos at a reasonable price, then for the church to organize itself, for a day to walk neighborhoods, handing out the Video, free of cost to anyone who would accept it. That same church was to follow-up in the neighborhood, inviting people to come to their church, to learn more about following this Jesus.

CHAPTER 13

BOB BROWN

I finally get to meet Bob Brown in person, we found that he and I were alike, both in a hurry to get as many people as possible told how to go to Heaven after death. This excellent Video was our vehicle to that means.

Bob and I had lunch to get to know each other better. What started that day lasted until first, Evelyn, then Bob went to their final reward, now spending eternity together in that same Heaven we were telling people about.

Robert E. (Bob) Brown became my dearest Friend and father figure. He taught me so much about what a Christian father, grandfather, husband, and friend should be like. He was a quiet gentleman of great courage. He not only told me and many others about Jesus, but he lived the life he told us about.

Bob was married to Evelyn; I rarely saw Bob without Evelyn unless we were out calling on Pastors about the Jesus video. But anytime we spoke in a church Evelyn was there to support us. Once a year they took their big motor home to Mazatlán Mexico to work as tourist missionaries there. When they started going, they would set up a TV by the vehicle and turn on the Jesus movie. Soon a crowd would be around watching the movie. That is how it started.

By the time years later, that they had to stop going due to health issues, there were many churches in that area, because two people, going into another land strange to them, told anyone who would listen about Jesus Christ.

The time Crystal and I went to Mazatlán, Mexico with Bob and Evelyn was such a blessing and an eye opener about how people live in other parts of the world. I had been to Mexico before and had seen much in the more poorer neighborhoods. However, I am forever amazed when there. We went to the one Christian church in the whole area at that time. Handed out Jesus Videos to people in the town and area around Mazatlan that tourist don't usually see. We learned how the workers in those tourist hotels etc. live. We visited the laundry that was out in the woods. It was three concrete tanks with water from a hot spring feeding it.

Ladies from the area were in the tanks washing clothes. The first tank was the soapy one with the second a rinse and the third used as the final rinse and child's bath tank. While we were there the women doing laundry were laughing and singing as they worked.

Then an older man, wearing only underpants, produced his only clothes in his arms. I thought poor Evelyn would surely be offended, but she handled it with the grace that Evelyn was known for so well. She laughed with and visited with the gentleman as if he were fully clothed.

Later when we were entertained by the Fiesta parade, complete with the dragon costumes and painted faces of death. Bob and Evelyn produced Christian tracts for handing out to anyone passing by. As the fiesta partygoers laughed and danced in the streets, they had silly string spray cans to spray as the parade progressed. Someone sprayed some silly string our way. Then the next thing we knew we were being barraged with sillystring in all colors. Evelyn had on a genuinely nice outfit with an expensive jacket. She also had her perfect hair done as usual.

The carnival folks were no respecters of her obvious classiness. In fact, I suspected she may have been the main target. But Evelyn laughed and joined in the fun for quite some time, continuing to hand out the well-received tracts about Jesus.

When the parade had finally passed our area, we looked at each other. We were all covered in silly string. We were also all still laughing when we got back to the Bob and Evelyn's Motorhome to get cleaned up. Many tracts had been given to people that night, but there was a cost.

Evelyn silky jacket was ruined with silly string fading into the material. She took it all in good humor though. I think that was probably the most memorable experience I ever experienced with

Evelyn. She demonstrated what a Godly woman could accomplish with a smile and joy, in the face of what could have been a horrible night. Had she not had grace and a genuine joy to share with the people who had received the many tracts about Jesus from us that night in Mexico. All because her attitude was not holier than thou reaction. Bob and Evelyn had a commitment to spreading Gods love, finding that was the more critical thing done that evening. No matter the cost.

Bob had not always been that way though. He had been the wild son of a Christian mother and Alcoholic father. After many years of prayer by his Mom, his father gave his life to Christ too. Bob did not follow until later.

But when Bob made up his mind to do something, nothing would stop him. So, when he became a Christian, he started to tell others at work. Finally, one man told him he would kill him if he said one more word about Jesus, another broke a coffee cup over his head. Eventually, however, the men Bob worked with came to respect his stand for Jesus.

Bob and Evelyn stood strong for Jesus, even though Cancer in later years took her life, Bob continued to tell people about Jesus and what excepting Jesus could do for them to anyone who would listen. Bob not only told you about Jesus, but his life also showed you what an experience with Jesus was like. Bob was my ultimate example to live by, while we are on this earth.

A few years later cancer also took Bob. While Bob was in the hospital, we would talk by phone. He was San Diego with me in Texas. We would speak, even at the end of his life. He always encouraged me, knowing his time was near.

Our last conversation, Bob and I talked about his soon going to heaven. Some of Bob's last words to me were, "I wish you were going with me." The most significant words I have ever heard!

Bob and I had been through the spiritual wars together and built an incredibly special bond. I miss you, my friend. Bob, give Evelyn a hug for me there in Heaven. I will see you again soon, up in the sky, my dear friend. Thank you for all the wonderful times together, all the gentle lessons you taught me, and all the things you did for me. I love you still Bob. I trust you and Evelyn are having a great time together now, In paradise with our Jesus.

CHAPTER 14

VICTORY IN SAN DIEGO

$\mathcal{W}$e could pass out as many videos to people as we could, as fast as we could. Even a person like me, as a new Christian, could hand this to anyone and know that they would have the complete biblical account, from the Gospel of Luke, of Jesus. Including an invitation to accept Jesus at the end.

I even put one on a friend's doorstep once, because I was too insecure about knocking on his door yet. We just needed to get many more people and churches on board with the project so we could be handing them out faster.

I was on fire like I have never been in my life! I thought, with my sales ability, I could get Pastors on board. They would then get their churches on board so we could cover all of San Diego, with the word of God.

Only two things were holding us back. I had no job, no money, and no credibility to walk into a church asking them for money to buy the Videos. Much less, get their churches organized to hand them out.

What is more, I had no way available to support myself and my wife while I did it. All I had to offer was a passion for serving Jesus, I realized later that God was leading my thoughts and actions. He would show me the way to do this if I just believed in His words.

Since that time, I have heard many people say they wanted to serve God, but when the actual costs were too much, they quit. Often, our material possessions keep us from serving God, even when we feel that call in our hearts. The Bible addresses this issue when it talks about the rich young man asking Jesus about following Him. Jesus told him to sell all he owned and give the proceeds to the poor, then come follow Him, Jesus. The young man left broken-hearted because the cost was too high. Some competent ministry people have been stopped in this same way. They are just more attached to their lifestyle than to be able to truly follow Jesus' plan for their lives.

For the last 25 years, I have served Him through Faith Ministry. Which means I have not been employed by any church or organization, except for a two-year stint with the National organization of 'The Jesus video Project of America.' A division of 'Campus Crusade for Christ. In return, God has supported my needs each of those years. Through donations made by people and churches who believed in me and what God was doing through his ministry.

During those years I have stumbled sometimes, but never so far, that God could not fix or forgive what I would mess up.

Bob and I started making plans.

CHAPTER 15

GOD STILL MOVES

I heard it said so many times that "I'm waiting on Gods timing," or "waiting on God to show His will," or better still "we are waiting on God to move or show us what He wants us to do." Hogwash! God is waiting for us to get off our knees and get on with His work. He is already there and working if we will but open our eyes, hearts, and souls to Him. Just start putting one foot in front of the other, God will lead us to His finish.

That is why Paul said in 2 Timothy; chapter four, verses two through seven, "Preach the Word!"

Be ready in season and out of season. Rebuke, convince, exhort, with all longsuffering and teaching. For the time will come when they will not endure sound doctrine, but according to their own desires, because they have itching ears, they will heap up for themselves teachers; and they will turn their ears away from the truth and be turned aside to fables. But you be watchful in all things, endure afflictions, do the work of an Evangelist, fulfill your ministry. For I am already being poured out as a drink offering, and the time for my departure is at hand. I have fought the good fight, I have finished the race, I have kept the faith." (NKJV).

Paul did not say, to stand around praying for guidance, waiting for God to spell out in advance, our clear path to some imagined victory out there someplace. Instead, he said that the plan we are waiting for has already been told to anyone listening.

The plan is given throughout the Bible! But here, in the verses above, it's very clear that instead of waiting, we are to be ready anytime to share the Gospel of the Good News, that God created the world and us, God sent His only Son, Jesus, to us to live with us awhile then to be killed by us for our sins or the wrongs we have all done at some time in our lives.

Jesus died a horrible death on the Roman cross. He did not have to, but He did, so you and I do not have to pay the price of our wrongs, throughout eternity. We can be changed from whomever or whatever we are, to another Paul, who will merely teach what is in the Bible as the truth. As God's plan continues to unfold before us even now.

Be watchful all the time, endure hardships, do the work of an Evangelist, fulfill your ministry. An Evangelist merely means to tell others about our Christian faith by telling them the 'Good News.' There are many tools available today to help us if we are too unsure of ourselves to speak the story of Jesus and how he changed our lives.

Just use the internet to look up the 'Jesus Film.' Play it for them. Also, many bookstores or websites, explain it to us. Just be sure of your source, it must reflect only the truth as said in the Bible.

Not just a person's views, without being backed up in that Bible. Otherwise, we may fall into the category of those who only hear what they want to hear from teachers who are just tickling ears or teach false fables instead of pure Jesus. So, beware! No matter the name or reputation of a writer, filmmaker, or speaker. Even preachers should always be checked against the Bible as the only source of proven words and ideas given by God Himself.

Some warned that even Paul had gone into the desert to learn before his ministry started. But I did not have three years, I needed to be at work right then!

Jesus Video gave me that tool to be able to do just that. Go to work, right now telling people about Jesus.

I was so hungry and enthused that in my hurry I made some mistakes. But I soon learned that Jesus honored my efforts and cleaned up my mistakes. He just needed me to take that one step to Jesus, he had people in place already to help me, I just did not know it yet.

CHAPTER 16

JESUS VIDEO PROJECT

*G*etting the approval from the San Diego office was not difficult once I met and received the support of Bob Brown, the businessman that the newspaper article was about that got me interested in the first place. I met with Bob a few times as we got to know each other.

He patiently listened to my enthusiasm and the plan growing in me to reach San Diego with the Jesus Video. The day came that the San Diego office assigned me to the part known as North County, part of San Diego County. Still a vast area to cover, nine hundred thousand people or three hundred thousand homes.

Once I had Bob's trust and the regional offices endorsement, Bob and I went to work. We called on Pastors all over the area together. Bob had the class, and I had the mouth, we both had a passion that was contagious enough that many of the Pastors listened to us and got involved. We were invited to many churches to speak. Usually, Bob deferred to me because he was a man of few words and a soft voice.

He had no idea how powerful those few words were, as we left one large church after I had given my story and dream of reaching the lost by giving the Video away, he quietly said to me. "I'm proud of you, I couldn't do that."

Wow! No one had ever said that to me before! I was humbled and pleased at the same time. In my eyes, the mighty Bob Brown had just approved of me. At that moment it did not matter to me that my bills were due or stacking up, nothing mattered except getting the job done and keeping the respect given to me by God and Bob. I knew then that I was on the right track.

I prayed a lot, talked to my wife about what was happening. Talking about Pastors actually saying yes to getting involved and having me to their church to get the congregation involved too. My wife said to me, "you do what God is calling you to do. I'll support you in it, we will trust God to provide what we need to live on above what I can make in my job."

Between all I was learning about God and Jesus along with the two statements by Bob and my wife, I became a minister of faith that day. We prayed and trusted God to show us our way and to somehow support us if we were genuinely doing His will. Moreover, God did. In so many ways.

Our neighbor Bill Budd stepped in then to change our lives again. He had met Bob at one of our functions and somehow contacted him about me being behind on bills and our trust in God to provide. Bob and his wife Evelyn, Bill and his wife Joyce, joined Crystal and me in praying for God's instructions as well as our support if we were genuinely obeying Him.

Both Bob and Bill's backgrounds when they were younger were much like mine. Maybe that is why they believed in me so much. I do know that God began supplying our needs, much from or through these two men who believed in me and encouraged me so much, as I started my long journey of working for Jesus.

From those days till now at the age of seventy-one, as I write this account, God has never let me down. I did not get into ministry to get rich, and I have not, but I have also never been without what was needed to care for my family. Yes, we have sacrificed some things, but we have received so many more and been blessed so much more than ever imagined in my life as you will discover later. Let me say right here that I do not recommend following the path I have unless you have prayed then prayed more. Be sure God is calling you before you take that step of faith. If you are confident in your calling, do not look back. To serve God is the most high calling, it will come with love, pain, suffering, sacrifice, and responsibility for your life and actions as well as the responsibility for sharing Jesus with those many peoples for their eternities that you will encounter along your path, but it will also give you a pure joy.

Slowly the Jesus Video Project of North County, San Diego, California came to life. As donations and supporters grew, so did the Project. We got an office to work from and a staff to handle the growth needs. We were not a one- or two-man ministry any longer but a thriving ministry with over sixty volunteers, being guided by a staff of four or five people. We started promoting our Project with press releases to radio, tv, Christian newspapers, radio adds, did interviews, put up billboards, yard signs, windshield covers, gave out church bulletin inserts, spoke in churches and word of mouth.

We began receiving donations from people and churches all over the area that wanted to reach North County with the Gospel of Jesus. I was amazed at the size of some of the gifts. I was invited to dinner at a couple's home one evening, as the evening progressed, we talked about the Project and my vision to spread the Gospel. As the evening ended, we were leaving when our host handed me an envelope, asking me not to open it until I was home.

Later, at home, I opened the envelope to see a check of twenty-five hundred dollars. Wow, our first official donor, I was ecstatic! I happily handed the check to my wife as I was praising the Lord for this first real gift for our vision.

I knew then that this was going to work, people and businesses would believe and follow us in raising the funds to buy the Video from the national organization, so we could give them, free of charge to families. Showing the love of Jesus and allowing people to accept Jesus Christ as their Savior and friend, to transform lives for eternity!

As I celebrated this glorious victory, my wife looked at the check and said I had better look again. My heart fell. I must have read it wrong; it must have said two hundred and fifty dollars instead. I looked again, it was a donation of not twenty-five hundred dollars, but twenty-five thousand dollars!

I could not wait to call my partner Bob Brown, at eleven o'clock at night, we rejoiced together on the phone for this first of many large donations we received.

As we grew, we began meeting with our many volunteers. We would meet every Thursday night with forty to sixty volunteers, hear their stories from the past weeks' efforts. Many weeks we received donations or commitments that had been given during the week., sharing, and praising God for the excitement from each week's efforts. It seemed like every week there would be increased results to celebrate as we continued to follow God's leadership.

Many churches were represented in a unified effort. One week a man said he had a check from a donor for one hundred thousand dollars! That was enough to mail a Video to every home in two or more of the areas we covered in North County.

Another time a man came to our office, I had never met before, but he and his wife had been at a church I had given the Sunday message at. It always included my testimony of Jesus transforming my life from a Texas drunk to a sober servant of His. It also added the Jesus Video, and how I now led the effort to give a free Video to every home in North County San Diego. The couple had been convicted strongly that day of helping as much as they could.

Their five-thousand-dollar check represented one of the most sacrificial gifts we ever received, I believe. They had cached in everything they could from savings, to selling off some items, so they could to raise money. The husband brought the funds to help "give the gift of Jesus' salvation to as many people as the funds would allow."

Then came the conversation one evening with Bob and Evelyn Brown. Over dinner, Bob, in his so quiet way, calmly said they had just sold a rental property and were donating the one hundred and fifty thousand dollars profit to the Project!

As news of our successes started coming to the public's attention through tv news and newspapers, about some of our events. As leader of the Project and spokesperson, I started getting offers from churches and organizations to work for them. A megachurch went as far as to actually offer me a salary and expenses if I'd come on staff to lead outreach.

This was after I had decided God was telling me to do a Tent Revival! A Tent Revival in Southern California? I must not have heard that right Lord. However, night after night the dreams of the revival came to me. Finally, I said, "Lord if you want a Tent Revival, you'll have to show me what to do." I do not have a tent or any experience, much less, I do not have the money it will take.

God kept showing me He had everything, all He needed was for me to be obedient. I tossed out the idea one day at a Pastor's luncheon to decidedly mixed reviews. However, I was surprised that Pastors, from different denominations, supported the idea. Some privately said they had wished for years that someone would try it but were afraid it would not go over in the San Diego area. Some were sure it would fail but would help me if I could put it together. God Got busy!

Our Thursday night meeting team listened with mixed feelings too, but in the end, as God started bringing ideas to them, people started responding. First two massive show tents, with the center post of 100-foot-tall, were made available. A price and way to rent them were offered. We had to put them up ourselves though. Then the mayor of one of the cities making up North County, offered to rent us some choice city land right by the freeway, for a three-day weekend. We were off and running, money came in to help finance it, we got a videographer to film it and a local, favorite Christian band to play for us.

I was stunned by God's answering, not only was I going to lead a revival, but God brought all the pieces together to do a real, old-fashioned Gospel revival, in Southern California! David, the kid from Texas, who had been a worm rancher, western wear salesman, restaurant owner, drunk, and bar fighter, was really going to do this? How could God use me this way?

Satan started talking to me too, "Who's going to listen to you after all you've done? You do not deserve to tell people they have sinned when you have sinned so much yourself!

Remember that time in Dallas when you got drunk with

your boss? You tore up the bar with him when you two fought everyone else in the bar? Your boss had to pay damages so they would not send you to jail that night. Then you go to that all-night eatery with your shirt torn nearly off, still drunk from the nights partying?

Before you even got out of your car, you had that woman open your car door, she started grabbing at your lap with one hand, while she picked your pocket with the other hand. She had that cigarette with those long ashes hanging loose in her mouth to distract you. You were too drunk to know what to do.

While you are distracted by the fact, she had only two front teeth, and the long ashes about to fall on your pants, she got all the money out of your pockets. You were such a sucker. Suddenly she was gone! As she disappeared into the crowd, you looked up, trying to spot her. As you were looking your eyes focused on the car parked across from you, right on your bosses' eyes, laughing at you, adding insult to injury.

Like a crazy man, you jumped out of your car to assault the crowd of men and women she had disappeared into. Screaming at them, convinced she was there still, hiding among them. Never realizing they were circling you, or that no one else in the crowd looked like you.

I nearly had your no-good soul that night! When those men closed in on you, I thought sure they would kill you. They were mine; you see? Organized thieves trained to rob and roll pathetic drunks like you, too drunk and too stupid to know you were in real danger. If God had not sent those police officers to save you, I would have had another soul that night.

Especially when you fought with the policemen! They even had to back you over the hood of your car, having to threaten you with that Billy club. Oh, what a drunken fool you were. You can't be an Evangelist, no one will take you seriously if they find out who you really are!"

God had another plan though, my past was part of what people came to hear, it gave me the ability to talk honestly with people that were broken or had histories of their own. Somehow our God has used my past to give me credibility with the men and women He would put in my path.

The Tent Revival was a victory, it overcame a sudden cold front that dropped temperatures to the thirties on our first night. We had no heaters as we were not expecting temperatures like that in San Diego, California. People were cold, some went to cars to retrieve blankets to wrap up in. Our crowd was small that first night, but when I gave the invitation, a few came forward any spite of the cold. Some also went to our second tent, the prayer tent.

The next day was our Saturday youth day, we had different Christian bands playing several types of music all day. We also had diverse kinds of youth show up. Most stayed for hours as the bands played with most of the musicians giving testimonies and mixing with the youth. Our prayer tent was busy too. We had several adults working in that tent, some with tables passing out literature of Bibles. Also, we had prayer leaders and counselors there. Late in the afternoon I gave a message and alter call again. And again a few came forward.

The evening service was warmer as we had rented portable heaters to place around the two tents. The word was getting out that we were there and that we were not a weird group, but a mix of local churches and the Video Project that had been getting the publicity.

We had two large Video screens on either side of us when the band played, they ended with an upbeat version of a favorite hymn. The drummer was the bandleader, his special solo nearly brought the house down it was so good. As his drums faded, I came to the microphone, to deliver the message God had laid on my heart. It was a magical night for me, with the music, screens that would show the crowd and clips from our Video to punctuate what I was preaching at that time.

It all came together as if we were professionals doing this kind of thing regularly. Gods spirit was with us that night! When the invitation was given, no one came forward this time. I was dumbstruck. Had I not said the right words, what happened Lord? I did my best, it was a beautiful service with the music, the lights, the Video screens, and the videographer had done a superb job of the whole program. Why had no one responded?

I went home with questions in my heart that night, we had all given our all that night. Lots of reflection was needed before the answer came to me that it was not about me or us or how hard we worked to give a show for God. It was about God and the people He would bring and convict, of His love and desire to know Him personally. The 'show' was a good thing, but only God can call a person to Him. My job was to tell people about God and His Son Jesus. Not to count numbers of how many He would call to accept Him.

On Sunday night we would not have the band or videographer. I had spent the afternoon in the main tent praying. When a sudden gust of wind came into the tent picking up one support post to swing it in a full circle that would knock a person out of the first few chairs around them. First one post then it would settle, and another would lift and start swinging in the circles.

I set on the stage and prayed. I did not know what else to do, I did see that we could not let people inside for tonight's service with these posts swinging around, post after post would repeat the action. There was the one-hundred-foot-tall center post that was encircled by several smaller posts that were the support posts for the outer part of the tent. These were the posts that were circling. As I was watching the posts, a lady came into the back of the tent.

She said, "I have seen what you're doing here, God told me to bring you this small donation to help with the costs." About this time, she noticed the poles that were acting so strangely. "oh, my goodness she said, you need some prayer. I am part of a prayer worrier group. Would you mind if we came tonight to stand in the gap for you while the revival is going on"? After we talked some, I said yes to the prayer team coming to quietly stand on the edge of the crowd to pray all through the evening.

The evening came, the prayer people came. The wind left; the posts did not move all night. And when the altar call was given several came forward for prayer and for accepting Jesus as their personal Savior. We had done it! What God asked us to do, we had done to the absolute best of our abilities. God had shown up!

The team came together again on Monday to take the tents down and clean the property. We then had a business meeting to review our victories and our expenses. We were seven thousand dollars short of meeting the total costs for the Tent Revival. But many had been saved, and many others renewed their walk with Jesus. All we needed now was to trust God to help us raise the last money for our budget to balance. That is when my dear friend, Bob Brown spoke up, to say he would write a check for the whole thing.

He did right then, and we were paid off. God had done what He told me He would do if I were just obedient. A real miracle had happened in Southern California, we were not supposed to be able to do a Tent Revival in that area of America because people would not come. *But they had come!*

CHAPTER 17

LIFELONG FRIENDS, MARIO'S STORY

*M*ario was born in Mexico but came to America with his parents at age one, his grandmother helped raise him in the Catholic faith. Mario started getting into drugs, gangs, and alcohol at an early age and that kept him from graduating high school. However, he had met his future wife while still in school.

Esperanza was a Christian, so he went to church with her

some, even though he was not interested in it, Mario was interested in her so where she was, he was. They married soon after high school, and as she to him through her faith in Jesus, it gave him a foundation he did not realize at the time. As they began their family, Esperanza took the kids to church with his blessings. She could do her thing, he would do his, which was drugs and gangs.

After the seventeen years of prayers and near breakups, Esperanza's patience paid off as God began to wear Mario down, though he did not know it was God at the time, he began to tire of the lifestyle he had chosen.

Tired of the drugs, tired of keeping up with the younger guys, he was just tired. He looked up a cousin of Esperanza that had been through the same kind of life but had changed. He had only recently given his life to following Jesus, Mario started looking for Jesus, asking questions of this cousin.

A friend asked him "what did you want to live for? Your family? Or end up in jail or dead?" At the time he was drunk, but he says it was like he heard the voice of God, coming through, telling him, he had his family, job, and business. Why would he want to keep doing what he was? At first, his wife did not believe his declaration of his changing his life, she had heard it so many times before.

The cousin would meet with Mario to share from the Bible, it started making sense to him. Then came the day Mario found out his son was praying for him and asking others to pray.

That was the final revelation God used to reach Mario in a way no one else could have. Mario was on fire to tell his friends about Jesus, but they denied him, telling him he would fail. Their words did not stop him though, Mario just wanted to share the love of God.

When I heard his story, my heart went out to him. He was

sharing with anyone who would listen, about the same Jesus that I was. So, after he spoke, I made my way to him. We talked that night for hours it seemed like. He wanted to serve but did not have the support that God had given me.

My first time to become an encourager to new Ministry people began with my new friend Mario Gonzales. I told him about Jesus Video, and he shared with me his desire to reach people for Jesus.

Little did we know that a deep, lifelong friendship would begin that night. Since then, in some of the places we were given the privilege to serve God in, I have trusted my life more than once to Mario and Jesus

Later Mario watched the Jesus Video and became convinced he wanted to show it in his native home of Tijuana, Mexico. His first showing of the Video was to his Grandma. She said 'yes' to Jesus.

We were encouraged by Mario's enthusiasm to help him acquire the equipment needed to spread the Gospel of Jesus to Mexico and southern California in areas we would not have been able to reach if God had not brought Mario and me together.

Our North County San Diego team hosted a "decadent dessert night" fundraiser. Inviting People, we hoped would give funds to further our Project. That evening we introduced our new young ministry partner, Mario. We told about his ministry and his desires for Mexico. We ask anyone that felt the urge to help us supply the needed equipment to make a special offering designated towards Mario's ministry. Helping make it possible to reach the people of Mexico and others by showing the Video outdoors with his own projector and sound system.

We had a special guest speaker to attract our audience. We served fancy desserts mostly donated by local bakeries. A full house showed up. We visited among the guests for some time before our guest speaker talked, then I got up to do the wrap up along with the request for Mario. The night was another remarkable success.

We raised funds for our ministry we had hoped for but also received designated funds enough to buy that Video machine I have talked about. Also, a man offered his portable sound system for our use. We were now able to give these to Mario's new ministry. We were warned that the bulb probably would not last more than a year if we used it outdoors because the dirt and moisture would burn it out. However, at last count, the projector and its original bulb along with the sound system were still working. It has been at least twenty years since the night of the fundraiser. God is so faithful. Those machines have been used many, many times in dirt filled, outdoor settings.

Often my friend Mario would invite me to one of his showings of the Video in apartment complexes, where alone, I may not have been welcome. He would set up the projector outside just using the side of a building as the screen. Mario and his team would often offer popcorn and soft drinks along with the movie. Always the invitation at the end of the film to accept Jesus as personal Savior was well received.

In Mexico, we would go many miles inland, where we sometimes had no electricity, to show the film. Flyers were distributed around the Oaxaca Indian huts in the area. At dark, people would start coming to see this film of Jesus in their local dialect. We would set up a white sheet, using PVC piping to stretch it with, often we had strings of lights that came out from the screen. For the invitation, the lights were turned on so people could see as they followed the lights to the waiting ministry leaders who talked with them about Jesus. The projector, sound equipment, and lights were run by portable generators we brought.

More than once Mario and I would go to an area of Tijuana with our equipment in my van to a Pastor's home and church. Both home and Church were in a rented two car garage. The Pastor's family lived behind a bed sheet strung up across a space large enough to sleep. The kitchen was a two-burner hotplate. The church was some folding chairs that took up the rest of the space available.

The Pastor rented this garage from the family that lived in the house attached. We would show the Jesus Film across the street in an empty lot. Down the block were the local house of prostitution and the regional gang headquarters. The gang would try to intimidate us or those who came to see the movie by firing off weapons close by or driving by in a car loaded with members of the gang slowly with their most sour looks.

Some were afraid to come or to stay if already there when the gangs got active. Often a few would stand on the street corner across from our lot to get the name of those who came or to intimidate others from entering. Still, we would have a crowd show up to see Jesus in Spanish. Then came the night a larger group of gang members took over that corner and stayed throughout the whole showing. At the invitation, one lone gang member came across the street to sit on the very front row to become a follower of Jesus.

Often it would be early morning by the time we would be driving back to the United States border. We were stopped one of those nights by the Mexican military on a long empty stretch of road. They had a small building of the side of the road with the military looking men carrying automatic weapons and looking very threatening when they stepped into our path, blocking us. We had just come from a Video showing inland, the van had all Mario's equipment

The men had us take the equipment out of the van and set it on the side of the road, while they searched our van. Mario, in Spanish, asked the leader to let him go into the shack to talk to the Officer in charge. As he got out of the van, he said to me to let him have whatever money I had on me.

He was in there what seemed an eternity with me under guard by those men and their big guns. After a while Mario appeared from the shack, as he came toward me, he said: "Let's get this stuff in the van as quick as we can!" When loaded, we got out of there before anybody changed their minds about letting us go with all that valuable equipment for whatever dollars Mario had paid the officer in charge. We did not get to stop in Tijuana for the street tacos we usually got on our way home, we had no money left.

Often when crossing back to the US, we would wait for a lengthy line of cars trying to get to our side of the border. Street vendors were going to all the vehicles with trinkets to sell. Occasionally a car would be pulled out of the line to be searched for drugs. Mario and his team still work in Mexico showing Jesus Video.

CHAPTER 18

FROM A TEXAS JAIL TO THE WHITEHOUSE

*O*ur leadership team became aware of a way we could mail the Videos into whole neighborhoods or entire cities. So, we started trying out the idea of raising enough support to do just that. The plan went over with the church, no matter their denomination, to work together in raising funds to mail the Videos to larger areas. The churches were to do the follow-up.

Our strategies of open showings in public venues like movie houses, outdoor tent revivals, and local tourist attractions, began to get noticed at the national offices of the Project. Resulting in me being invited to join the national team to promote our ideas in a regional area of the USA.

From there, they promoted to National Field Director, representing the Project with a staff, including another four men, to reach America with our strategies. As the new National Field Director for the Project, I was honored to lead the men and our supporting staff at the national offices with the goal in the mailing of the Jesus Video to the entire United States. We also had the opportunity to mail a Jesus Video to every congressman and senator, along with each chief of staff. Working in Washington, I met with many of our Nation's leaders of politics and Ministries who had offices there.

This gave a country boy access to many very wealthy and powerful people who supported our Video outreach. Soon I was being interviewed on tv and radio about what we were doing. This came with many speaking opportunities to share my testimony or preach to audiences across our great Nation.

The theme of "It's a long way from a Texas jail to the Whitehouse," gave me the chance to share the story and love of Jesus with His forgiving heart to many people across this great country. To share His willingness to Transform anyone who asks and trust Him. For this, I will be eternally grateful.

For a man of my background, to be allowed, by God, to do these things was beautiful. But at each speaking opportunity, I would see a group of people that stood out. People wanting to hear more. Wanting to be used by God, to reach more people about Jesus, often with no one to lead or encourage them to take that first step. Many Pastors do not know how to or are too busy, to be supporting those who are saying 'Here I am, send me,"

I have learned that many warriors are discouraged from working for Christ because their leaders do not really know how or will not take the time to teach them, to win the lost to Jesus. It is too easy to be swept up in the running of a ministry and the needs of those in our flock, to focus time for those that would help us or be out winning the lost if they were just equipped or allowed to help.

It becomes too easy to tell ourselves we can do it all instead of spending time teaching or explaining to others in God's world, to help in ways that would allow them to share in God's glory.

How many more could we have accept Jesus if we leaders just opened up our hearts to equipping a team? Instead, we spend so much time on budgets, meetings, or preparing messages for Sunday that tell our flock what they should be doing in life. Often without showing them how to be an effective winner of the lost and hurting people around our churches.

I have been told since those days that our national team were responsible for mailing something over ten million Jesus Videos to homes across America. I just know that God allowed us to mail to whole States and many cities and neighborhoods, with the partnerships of many who gave to our Project in both small and substantial amounts.

God used donations like the one little lady gave me, six rolls of pennies she had saved. I was reminded of the 'widow's mite' mentioned in the Bible. God used the one-dollar donations just the same as He used the million-dollar contributions. It was humbling to be watching when God was at work.

It had been a long time since I had been involved in the Bible study that told me to "look where God is working and join him there." But what a ride It was!

CHAPTER 19

STEVE SVITECK...CRUSHED ALIVE!

Ａew volunteers came along, some with outstanding stories of God transforming their lives as well. One such was Steve Sviteck, here is his story:

"I got run over by a school bus. In 2009, on Easter morning. I have a brain injury, and I am not as lucid. I am not as cognitive as I was. For me to even string a sentence together is hard. It depends on how tired I am. I am kind of tired today.

I was drafted by the Oakland Raiders in 1970. I just played there for the preseason. I ended up with the Buffalo Bills where I finally made it to the traveling squad. I was not a great player, just an average player and I was lucky to make the team. I finished the year there and went back the next year which would have been '72 to start the season. I damaged my ankle bad in training, so they sent me back to Buffalo and took me down to the Mayo Clinic. The answers from Mayo was not good. The coach said we need to play football now, not next year and you have a bad injury there.

I went home and like my Dad, I got a job. I was going to work for the rest of my life just like everybody else. About a week later the phone rang. It was the Canadian football league. They said we drafted you extremely high and you did not want to come. You wanted to be an Oakland Raider, so how about now? Are you interested?

I said, "I'll see you next week." I went to Canada, and I did an excellent job there. I beat out everybody they had. I ended up as their starting middle linebacker! We played twenty-three games and went to the Super Bowl up there, which is the Gray Cup.

When you play professional football, alcohol, drugs, and women are always available, and I was not a Christian, so I hung out with the party guys. I had a weakness all throughout high school, college and professional ball leagues of being a weekend partier.

After the game, the rest of the weekend is a party. I was always on a winning team, so we did a lot of partying and everything that goes with it. There are different drugs and all kinds of things that got me going, but amid all the parties I got married, and that was the end of my football career. I went down to Phoenix, Arizona to visit with my brother-in-law and got into the business. I started making a lot of money. I got into recycling and built up quite a business. I was in that for over 10 years. I made millions of dollars, had my own airplane and flew all over the Country as I became about the largest recycler of paper in the USA. I think my football experience helped me because I learned what it is to compete, to push yourself.

My weakness is not drugs, it is drinking. When I drank, I did what everybody else did, whatever that was. It finally led to becoming an alcoholic, ending up in a lot of bad situations.

There were brushes with the law, sleeping in trees or under

docks. Once I was arrested for running down the streets naked. Eventually, I lost the business.

At one point, I came out of a detox center and as always, went right straight to the liquor store. I bought a bottle and came out. It was hot in Phoenix, so I was looking for shade, there was a trash truck that had the back door open. I climbed up in that trash truck, sat down, and drank part of that bottle, and I laid over and went to sleep. I had not had enough to pass me out or anything, I just relaxed.

Next thing you know, I woke up and did not know where I was at. I heard a lot of metal clanging and banging. I was in the back of that trash truck. It started to crush me. Being the first trash in, it crushed me for two hours and forty-five minutes. A lot of trash, a lot of pressure, bones breaking, I was in and out of consciousness. Every time that pressure came, it would press, and then it would stop. What I remember about that was it was very, very painful.

It dumped me out at a commercial dump. They have these great big caterpillar-like things that have huge spikes on them. They run over the trash after its dumped and smash all the air and break the pallets, smash the barrels, whatever is in the trash. All I remember is I knew that I needed to go somewhere. I remember crawling, trying to get out of where I was. I was in a bread loaf of trash they had pushed out of the back of the truck.

My head popped out of the top. I looked around and realized I was at a dump. One of these massive machines came at me. I could see that it was going to run over the trash that I was in, that 8-10 feet high loaf of trash was going to be compressed. I threw myself off the top, I hit the river rock and gravel. That thrasher ran over the garbage, as it did it took the bottom of my foot off. I tried as hard as I could to get away without it getting more of me.

It took my heel and the bottom of my foot completely off, pushed it down into the ground, sand and gravel, it was like river rock. I survived, but I did not know what was going on.

Then came another one of those machines, this one was coming right directly at me. The ground was shaking, and this one was going to run right smack over me. Naturally, I wanted to get out of the way. I tried to get up and discovered my leg broken. The one I tried to get up on first just rolled over, and I sank down.

The bones started squirting out of my legs because they had splintered. I tried to hold my leg together and the bones impaled into my hands. I just sunk down with the bones going into my hands, the bone tips were sharp, very sharp. It was excruciating. I tried the other leg; it would not work. Nothing would work. The thrasher kept coming, I did not have time to do anything. I knew I was done. I was a dead man.

I do not know how I did it, but I thought quickly enough to lean over forward toward the machine so that it would get my head first. My legs were already crushed, so I did not want it to roll up my body. I wanted it to get my head first, get the pain over with. I laid forward, and the ground was shaking and here came that big machine.

That is the last I remember. Later I found out, that somehow the machine operator had seen something move. He had stopped the machine to check out the movement and found me.

The paramedics had been summoned; they were cutting my clothes off. My shirt, my pants, my shoes, with big cutting things. I ended up in the hospital.

I almost died a couple of times. I was in there for 30 days, enduring several operations with a lot of screws and steel plates. After the 30 days, they sent me out of there. They wheeled me to the back door, handed me a bottle of ibuprofen, a couple of crutches, and said: 'see you later.'

I was just a drunk, a street person to them. I was in Phoenix, Arizona, no family, no friends, nobody. I was back out on the street. I started crutching down the street.

A kind nurse, that knew about me, stopped, pulled over and said "come on getting in. You can come over to my house and heal up." I do not know why she did that, but I thought it was great. I went to her house.

She worked the swing shift, so every time she would go to work, she would put the TV on a channel, and I did not have a remote. I had casts clear up to my knees, the cast came over my knees on one leg, so I could not walk. I had to use crutches; those casts were heavy in those days. Great big bumpy casts that everyone signs. Nobody signed mine.

I was stuck with the channel my host put the tv on. One day 'Jesus Video' came on. I watched it, in the end, I was thinking, Jesus is pretty cool. He is got a lot going there. I started thinking He had something to do with God.

When I had been on the streets, God sent a fallen Christian, now living on the streets too, he had led me to the Lord. He bugged me and told me I needed Jesus every single day. Finally, I said, "ok, it sounds good to me." He prayed for me. But I did not really understand at the time. When I saw the Jesus Video, that was my beginning, realizing that God existed, and He had sacrificed in the form of Jesus Christ for me.

Once I realized I was saved, the Lord led me to church. I started going to church, I have never looked back. That drunken Christian and the kind nurse with the tv on the Jesus Video gave me eternity with Jesus. By just believing in Him and asking Jesus to lead my life from that time on.

It shows us that God can use anybody to tell about His Son Jesus. Today I have everything I always wanted. From being a pro football player to having had money, an airplane, a big business. I made millions of dollars after football in my recycling, exporting, trucking company, but I was unhappy in the end. Empty."

Just because Steve has lived for Christ Jesus since those days, it does not mean he or we, are protected from life's happenings. It just means we know how to deal with those things differently.

Steve was going to the beach on Easter morning 2009 to help a friend, who releases hundreds of white doves at the Easter morning service every year. Steve was on his way to the State Beach, sitting at a red light at 6:45 in the morning, He was at the bottom of a hill coming off the freeway when a city bus plowed over him. He woke up in the hospital again, this time with brain damage. He has been fighting his way back for ten years now.

After the accident, Steve could not walk or talk basically. He could not work, did not use a computer. He could not even use a cell phone, could not communicate with anybody.

He did not even know who his neighbor was. He looked right at him, asking, 'Who are you?' It took about two and a half years for his brain to begin recovering. Our brain cannot recover as quickly as our body can. Our minds just take more time.

Today Steve continues to heal. He speaks at men's Bible study groups and much more. Steve is one tough man, to have survived the battles he has been through. His faith in Jesus Christ has made him one tough believer too. The Devil has tried to shut Steve up many times but failed each time. God will call Steve home one day, to give Steve his reward! But do not look for it anytime soon. Steve is not through telling others about Jesus and His Love.

CHAPTER 20

GOODBYE CALIFORNIA

*I*n 2001 I left the Jesus Video Project; I felt the days of Videos were about over. Feeling Gods call to move forward with the founding of 'American Renewal Movement.'

With my contacts in Los Angeles, we were able to produce two DVDs. One, about the 911 tragedy. It featured the wife of one of the pilots who died on that day. God had plans and people for us to meet yet.

As we moved back to the San Diego area, we were caught up in our first California fire. Waking up about three o'clock one morning to the smell of smoke. Looking outside, the red glow across the night could mean only one thing. There was a raging forest fire close to us, it was in the canyons behind us. Waking the wife, she started packing what could be taken quickly. While I and made sure the neighbors were all alert to the situation.

We turned our motorhome around, parking it in the driveway ready for a quick evacuation if needed. We loaded our dogs and the few possessions we could in the motorhome. With the wind blowing in our direction, we could smell the wood smoke, mixed with sparks in the air already. This being our first fire we did not know just how fast one can move as it creates its own wind, so we jumped in the convertible to see just how close the fire was.

We very quickly learned that evacuation does not include sightseeing. In just a few blocks we could see the monster coming up out of the canyons. The sky grew brighter, a red-orange, ominous glow, becoming a living thing, with its own power. We turned down a side street to get a better look, wanting to judge how close it was. Now we could begin to feel the heat from the still unseen flames.

Thankfully, we turned around, so we were facing away from the approaching fire. Before I could get out of the car to investigate further, cars suddenly came speeding out of the canyons.

One slowed enough to yell to us to get out, the fire right behind them. Jumping back into our car, I turned my head to see behind us.

I experienced the most terrifying thing I had ever seen. The fire burst out of the canyon, with a wind, creating its own tornado of flames! It looked like the fires of Hell, reaching out for us with nothing in its way.

We got out as fast as that little red convertible could go. Back home to join our neighbors in fighting to save our properties from being destroyed. We could hear explosions as propane tanks blew up. Ammunition went off as the fire got to it. The glowing cinders were carried on the wind to start new fires. Some on the neighbor's property.

We fought with garden hoses to put out small fires started by the cinders before they could spread. We struggled to wet down our propane tanks and rooftops. The fires raged around the area.

Miraculously the fire spared all four of our houses on the short road we lived on.

After the fire, we learned of one young couple that did not make it out in time. The young couples burned-out car was a stark reminder of just how fast the fire was moving. They had died just in the area where we had been, the fire swept over them and their car before they could get away from it.

As we spent the night wetting everything we could, neighbors helping neighbors as the fire burned one home after another in our area, yet missing houses right beside burned out hulls of someone's home.

We had rented the home we lived in at the time of the fire, along with its two acres, there was a beautiful orange grove across the country lane.

Judy and Randy Harmon managed the property for another person. Randy and Judy became then and are still close friends and supporters, both personally and of our ministry for many years now. Even after we moved back to Texas, we stayed friends, visiting each other's homes, helping each other when in need of prayer. It is the kind of friendship that sees a person through good times and tough times. When my wife and I divorced after moving back to Texas, Judy and Randy called from California, most faithfully, to get me through those dark days.

My brother was extremely ill, as was my Mother, both in Texas. My sister was there trying to care for both, Mom alone was a full-time job. My sister called to ask if I could come home to help with my brother as he was going to rehab in a nursing home. My family had an unspoken vow, to not let each other down if we were needed.

We made the decision that it was time to go back to Texas. It was one of the hardest decisions of my life. We had done well in

California, we had many friends, and my Nephew, whom we had helped get set up in California when he came from his home in England was there. We were close, it would not be easy to leave so many loved ones behind. To leave our ministry team, to restart the ministry in Texas was an unknown too.

I decided it was time to go home now. Back to Texas, where so much had happened in my former life, I wondered if any of my old enemies would still be there. Could I make a new life? Could God continue to use me in His ministry, where I had been in so much trouble? Would He bless me there, as He had done in California?

We said our goodbyes to our many friends in California with the thought that we would get my things in Texas settled and be back to California. God had other plans.

CHAPTER 21

TEXAS

*R*andy and Judy helped us as we loaded everything, we could get into a sixteen-foot cattle trailer and the back of our 6-cylinder pickup that would have to pull it. Our German Shepard and two Shiatzus in the cab with us. Said our final goodbyes and off we were on our unusual journey back to Texas.

We intended one last adventure through parts of California, Arizona, and New Mexico as we traveled. My first lesson came when we were in the mountains of California still.

We are driving the pickup truck and its heavily loaded trailer, with no trailer brakes, going up and down mountain roads.

As we began our first steep downward mountainside with a sharp curve in it. We got our first lesson in mountain driving with a heavy trailer with no brakes.

A pickup will slow as its brakes are applied. However, those same pickup brakes will not slow a sixteen-foot stock trailer full of weight behind you. Therefore, said trailer has no way to slow down just because you, in the pickup, want it to. The result is the trailer, going faster than you in your truck, will suddenly try to pass by you on one side or the other.

The more one tries to stop or slow down, the more likely the trailer will either beat you to the bottom of that mountain by reversing rolls with your truck, pulling it down the mountain.

However, it chooses to go, either by leading you down the road or by creating its own path, over the mountainside's edge.

Either, are not an acceptable choice, as the result of one is a sudden fall into the tops of those trees you have been admiring, way down below. The other is an extremely wild ride backward down the mountain that cannot end happily.

The right answer is to go very slowly down in a low gear with minimum brake use. And did I mention? Pray like crazy that you do not see that trailer pass you! Now I did not know that rule of the road until we had to outrun our trailer down the first steep mountain we came to.

Sometimes it felt like it would overtake us to win the race and sometimes, it would be content to just do its best to push us off the side of the mountain. I am sure though that was the tallest mountain in the world because it felt like an eternity before getting down it alive. That was a harrowing way to learn, though it is certainly not recommended. Just add trailer brakes to your trailer, before you start a trip.

That journey included going to look for turquoise mines out in the desert while still pulling the trailer behind us. Once getting stuck in the sand or another time hitting high center with the trailer on one side of the high spot and our truck on the other side.

We finally made it to Texas, again with a plan to take some time off from ministry before anything else. I still had contact with the Jesus Film people, which were a different team than the Video Project had been. The Video Project had gone out of business a couple of years after I left, as the Video era ended, to be replaced with DVDs.

Through my contacts, I had the rights to market the Jesus DVDs to some major USA Ministries, one would use it in teaching English to foreign students on college campuses. This kept my income alive, while I took that break.

One of life's little turns took place during the break, as I was arrested for an unpaid fine, from ten years before when I had lived in Texas. A result of my old life. I honestly believed I had paid off the fine, but, without a receipt, I had no proof. So, when I was invited to the city offices to talk about it, I did not hesitate to go. I had been in California serving God for those ten years. I had been clean and sober all that time. I was used to being respected. But when I arrived, I was instantly put in handcuffs and arrested. For a ten-year-old 'outstanding warrant.'

Afterward, the detective explained how I was found so soon after moving home, I did not live in the same county as the warrant even. Hence the phone call and polite request I come into talk about the warrant. You see, they needed me to come into their county to serve the warrant. In other wards, they had to trick me so they could arrest me inside the county the offense took place.

I had come to town with my brother that day. The detective was kind enough to escort me, in handcuffs, across the street so I could tell my brother that I would not be going home with him.

Instead, I want back to jail, where I had sworn never to be again. I sat in the holding tank, which is a larger cell with a bench around three sides. The fourth side was cell bars. I found a place on a nearly full bench. Nobody really talked to one another. Probably because we were all embarrassed to be there.

I was better dressed than the others as I had planned to do other things in town with my brother that day. I only mention this because, being different, caused me to be a curiosity to some of the other men dressed in work clothes. We all quietly waited for our name to be called. Hoping to see a judge or bail bondsman.

I realized I was being stared at by one man. Every time I would glance his way, he would be staring at me in a most unfriendly fashion. I thought, oh no, I am going to have to fight that man soon if I do not get out of here. I could see in his eyes he was working himself up to it.

It had been over 10 years since I had a fight. My bar fighting days were well past me. God had changed my life while in San Diego.

Just when he was ready to come after me, God intervened, my name was called. Brother had alerted my wife and my son. Both were at work, so the daughter in law and grandchildren were there to see me. That was the most embarrassing moment of my life, I believe.

Looking through a jail window at my grandkids. Wide-eyed and confused to see grandpa in jail, they told me my sons' family was going to pay my fine to get me out of jail. I did not understand at the time why my wife had not come instead of my son's family. We had the money coming the next day from a recent DVD sale.

Soon I would though, as I went through a heartbreaking divorce. Just as I about to restart the 'American Renewal Ministry.' I realized I was soon to be no longer married again. I feel as if the spouse of a minister is often living in what has been called the bubble, where the spouse and family are expected to be perfect, according to the world's standards. This takes a toll on a lot of ministry marriages.

I have struggled with depression my whole life, even while traveling to the Washington DC scene, or speaking throughout the USA. I felt like if anyone found out who I really was they would not want anything to do with me. I just was not good enough to mix with people I had been with or to have the position I had.

When my wife left, I fell into a terrible and dark depression again. I thought that the ministry was over as well as marriage. If I could not handle my own family, how could I deserve to represent Jesus to others? My life was over without those two things. That was my life. First, I tried drinking one night, thinking that if a bad boy were what she wanted, I would just go back to that life.

The more alcohol consumed the more self-pity was felt. Until it was decided I should just to end my life. Taking my shotgun, I put the barrel in my mouth, putting my toe on the trigger.

I sat there for a very long time, wrestling with Jesus and Satan. Satan saying push the trigger, Jesus saying He still wanted me to work for Him. Even now, years later, I can feel that tug of war again as I write this. It was a horrible time in my life, removing the shotgun long enough to call a friend in California who prayed for me.

Again, God intervened, my son, knocked on the door. Coming to check on me. He saw the shotgun and at once understood what was happening. He began at Once, gathering up my guns and knives to take with him.

As I sat there watching, I kept thinking, yes but you did not remember my antique pistol up in the closet. Running out of beer is a disaster for a drunk. The insane craving for more will drive us to irrational thoughts and actions we would never consider when sober.

I still wanted to find the guy my wife was with, thinking I would kill them both, in my drunken mind, logic was thrown out the window.

Grabbing the old pistol, being sure it was loaded, I started walking to my son's house. With a grin in my heart, because I had the gun and I knew where that old truck, that I had bought for one hundred fifty dollars so long ago was parked. My son and I had traded it back and forth to each other for years, and, it did not need a key to start it.

It had been parked because the transmission was leaking fluid.

Of course, that did not enter my mind either at the time. I snuck up quietly, so my sons' dogs would not hear me and start barking to alert him that anyone was around.

It was after midnight by now, so I figured all would be asleep anyway. If I could start the truck, I should be able to get away before anyone could stop me. Opening the door,

I slid in, closing the door silently. All was going great so far; I turned the ignition. Vroom! The truck started; I had forgotten how loud it was with no mufflers. Just straight pipes on it, Wow, it seems loud.

Hurriedly dropping the gearshift into drive and giving it the gas, I was going to be out of here before they could wake up even! Nothing! Except a loud roar, no movement at all. I quickly shifted to neutral then reverse. Again, no movement, dropping it in low gear, a roar went from the loud pipes. No movement at all, not even an inch.

There is a tap tap tap on the side window. Turning to the noise, I looked into my son's eyes. Shaking his head, no, while opening the door. "No Dad," he says. "No transmission fluid in the truck for weeks, where do you think you're going anyway?" Then he saw the pistol in the seat.

Back to my place we went, he reminded me that the old gun blew fire and the cap from the bullet, out the back, if the pistol was fired. It would have done more harm to me than anyone else. My son spent the rest of the night on my couch, sleeping between my bed and the door. Ensuring that Dad did not do anything else stupid that night.

After sobering up the next day, to the shame and regret. My son posted my granddaughter's picture on the inside of the front door, to remind me, why I did not commit suicide or try another night of drinking and stupidity. That was the last drink of alcohol I have ever taken.

Shamefully asking for Jesus Christ's forgiveness for my slip and mindset that even caused me to want to drink was difficult. Needing much soul-searching. The shame came from letting down my God and my son's family.

I had been a Christian leader and representative for Jesus to many people across this Country. Yet in my crisis, I had turned to worldly things instead of really trusting God to get me through the trials in my life. I matured a lot in my walk with Jesus in the coming days, by examining my beliefs and my faith. I needed to decide if I honestly believed in God and His Son Jesus Christ. If so, would I live up to what I had told others?

Would I prove, through my life, what a walk with Jesus was to be like? The answer was yes. I recommitted my life to strived to live a life that God could be pleased with. You see, my mistake came when I forgot God and His Son Jesus are whom I had represented myself as serving. Not my now ex-wife or even my son.

My life was not to be wasted by pushing a shotgun trigger. Jesus had not forsaken me, only a person, had let me down.

CHAPTER 22

A RESTART

*A*fter my fiasco with drinking again, I asked forgiveness and for Gods plan for me now. He answered through a friend, who said he would not feel sorry for me, but he would help me. He did several things, like meeting for coffee often and getting me into a Christian counselor. The counselor helped me through the pain of having been heartbroken by the loss of yet another marriage.

I cannot really blame anyone I guess, life with me has not quite been easy on marriages. After being married to four different women, I began to suspect the problem was with something I was doing wrong, rather than the wives.

That counselor, met with me several times, hearing my story of marriages and divorces, then he gave me the hard truth. "David, I think your problem is that your picker is broken" My what is broken? "Your picker," he said again.

He went on to explain that I picked people to marry that I wanted to help by fixing their problems. In fact, I had in hindsight done just that. He went on to tell me that I should do the 'fixing' in my work, not in a marriage. He told me, If I ever married again, it should be to someone that I came home to for comfort and simple enjoyment. Someone that supported me and my work. Not someone that I needed to 'fix.'

I was encouraged to join a singles group at church, soon I started making friends, both men, and women. We did things together a lot of weekends.

Then I heard that a mission group from the church was going to go down to the hurricane Katrina area, cutting trees that had fallen on houses or blocking roads, etc. It was to be led by my friend, so I asked him if I could go, even though I was not a member of his church. The answer was yes.

I found a chainsaw and started doing ministry again right then, I just did not know it yet. We cut trees for hours each day we were there. Not long afterward another hurricane hit Texas, back we went to cut more trees and help clean up the areas we could.

This time I saw the help that strangers from all over the Country were coming to give, from people like us to the folks who had loaded up a cooker and food supplies on their truck.

They headed to the storm area with no plans other than to feed whoever God showed them to feed. From the relief workers to local people that would be hungry. They started by setting up in the middle of a street, the only place they could find due to the destruction left by the storm. Opening free feedings to any and all. Soon others came to volunteer to help them. When I was there, they were feeding hundreds per day. God was using one couple to work where no one else was, to minister to the hurting and hungry.

Other churches, regardless who they were, began to show up, to build cabins for temporary shelters, to clean up areas, to just listen to the stories of those hurting from losing everything from loved ones to homes and businesses. I learned about disaster relief ministries there.

Soon after a small town, close to my home, had a devastating fire that burned down churches, homes, and business.' I felt Gods prompting to go help, wherever I could. He guided me to take Bibles and a book to help people recover from the losses that filled with scripture.

I could go into the hardest hit areas. Talking to a rancher who only had a few cows and a steel corral left of his home place. He was covered in ash blackness but was still thankful he and his family had survived. Like so many others, he had lost the families Bibles in the fire that destroyed so much. I offered that tough rancher a Bible and was rewarded by his tears of thankfulness. While we stood at his corral. With one foot up on the bottom rail, of all that was left. Even his tractor was burned beyond repair. But he and his family would now be able to reread Gods words of comfort.

Noticing one day that there were a lot of my single friends that were alone at the holidays. I picked a date and location, got out the word, I would be there for coffee and conversation if anyone wanted to come. Several showed up, the 'American Renewal Ministry' was restarted that night and grew from there.

It grew quickly enough we soon changed locations to accommodate. Then we split into two different nights to meet unique needs. They still grew. God was at work! We were able to help parents of kids in drug use and much more. As word of mouth got out, more came.

This went on into years of working with marriages, drugs, jail, prison, even suicide rescues, and long-distance phone relationships to help hurting people in other places.

We opened a resale shop to employee some of those needing jobs. We were able to employ many of those who were recovering their lives for assorted reasons. We also reached a lot of our customers for Christ. It was a wonderful experience. However, God was still looking out for us, even when I did not understand at the time why things were happening as they were. We lost our lease on the building after a few years, when a new owner of the property we leased, wanted our spot for a retail store of their own. It was a massive job to sell our inventory down, then to dispose of what had not sold and clean up the property.

However, only a couple of months after we closed the store I had a stroke. If we hadn't closed when we did, Darlene would have had to go through all the closeout sales and cleaning up our warehouse by herself.

While I was on one of the trips to the two Texas hurricanes, I noticed one evening that everyone except me would get a call from or would call loved ones at home. I had no one I needed to call every day. Then one night my cell phone rang. It was one of the ladies from our singles department. Calling to see if I was doing ok. It really touched my heart that she cared enough to track down my brother to get my number. Just to call because she felt that I was alone. I guess that call was the first of many kind things this lady did for me that began a friendship that would eventually result in our marriage. And guess what? She did not need to be fixed but just shared from her heart.

CHAPTER 23

DARLENE

*M*y divorce was finally over, I was down, but I went to church with my brother on Sunday. I just did not want to go to the singles class, I did not want to explain anything to anyone. So, I helped in the kitchen during class time.

Darlene had missed me, she asked my brother where I was, he explained where and why.

I looked up from my work when she came into the kitchen. Darlene did not talk or ask foolish questions; she just came over and gave me a friendly hug. She told me it would be all right, then she left. Not intruding in my privacy but encouraging me with Gods love from a friend.

After a time, we started sitting together in our class on Sundays. Often our whole class would go out to eat after church. One Sunday after we had known each other quite a while, we were leaving from one of those lunches at the same time, so I walked her to her car. As I shut the car door, it was all I could do to resist leaning down to kiss her goodbye. Instead, I asked her if I could call her sometime, or would she be interested in going out to dinner someday? The answer was yes. I called the next few days to ask her out, again the answer was yes.

We went to dinner and talked for a long time. Darlene says I spoke of my whole past. But I had the idea that she would not like me if she knew who and what I had been. I wanted to get it over with, so I would not get into a relationship with anyone that would then leave that relationship when they found out about my past. Darlene did not seem phased, that left me so shaken that I left my credit card at the restaurant when we left. I had to go back the next day for it. Only twice has she rattled me enough to not know quite what I was doing.

The other time was after dating awhile I got up enough nerve to kiss her goodnight as I was leaving. As I went in for the kiss, she came into my arms. Our lips met; I was in for the shock of my life. She went to her tiptoes, made a soft sound down deep in her throat and her soft lips melted into mine. I did not want it to end. I said good night in a stunned frame of mind.

She closed the door, I made my way to my truck thinking 'wow, what was that? I sat there for a few minutes recovering from being kissed better than I had ever experienced. Finally, I got out of the pickup. Walked back to her door, knocked. Darlene opened the door a little surprised to see me back. I asked' do you think we could do that again?' We did.

We went to New York on a mission trip with other people on the team. It was snowing in New York. Central Park was beautiful. One day as we men were working on a homeschool, we needed some part we did not have. Another man and I went to get it at a local store. As my friend was paying out, I noticed this little box of ninety-nine cent rings that looked like diamond engagement rings. On a lark I bought one, thinking it would be funny to give it to Darlene as a pre-engagement ring.

On some off time, she and I went to see Central Park. We got there to find it hard to go anywhere due to the snow covering everything. We did follow a trail made by others to an area with a bench and a creek running. I brought out with my ring and tried to get Darlene to sit on the snow-covered bench. But she says, "no way she is sitting in that snow to get the back of my pants all wet." I hand her my joke ring explaining it is a pre-engagement ring. Well, on her finger it goes. It is no longer a joke but the real deal to her.

The missions team had lots of fun at my expense with my cheapskate ring. The only problem with the ring incident was that Darlene took it very seriously and did not take it off. It was amazing how long the Silver coloring stayed of the little ring. She keeps it in her jewelry box today.

Later, I gave her a real ring. We did get married. Our vows said among other things that we would love each other in good and bad days, as well as in sickness and health. Little did Darlene know then, that she would be called upon to prove she meant that part of the vows for the rest of our lives.

We had not been married long when she got the call that I had flipped our car three times, they were still working on getting me out of the car. A friend brought her out to the accident just as I was finally being removed from the wreck to be put on a stretcher. A helicopter waited nearby in a field to care flight me to the hospital. As they got me on the stretcher, she came to kiss me before they loaded me up.

I was heavily loaded up with morphine by that time. The medical people on hand had cut my pants off I guess because I looked into her eyes, very romantically and said, "at least I have clean underwear on, as Momma taught me."

Somehow, through the tears, she laughed, I had been in the car around three hours, they tell me, by the time I was extracted. All I remember was seeing a telephone post right in front of me as the car came out of one ditch to fly a hundred twenty some feet to the other side of the road. I said a quick prayer asking God not to let me hit that telephone pole.

The car flipped as it landed, went over again, then did a half flip that landed me on the drivers' side down. I remember feeling the car sliding for what seemed forever, but it came to a stop, with the wheels facing that telephone post. I was about thirty inches away from it when the ride finally was over. The engine was still running, I could smell gas. Afraid the car would blow up with me in it, I managed to turn off the key part way at least, so the engine went quiet.

I could not move anything but my arm. I was only half conscious, but I knew that the engine must not keep running. Being on a country dirt road, that was not traveled this time of day much, I was in and out of consciousness. After a while, I realized

I could open the moon roof of the car still and might be able to at least wave someone down if they came by.

After a time, a man drove past. As he did, he thought, 'that car was not there when I went to lunch.' He looked again, this time he saw my hand waving out the moonroof.

Again, God had spared my life for some reason known only to Him. The emergency medical team flew me by helicopter to the hospital, they were sure I had internal injuries. I had no blood cuts or apparent outside damage.

Tests showed that I had three fractured lumbar in my lower back. But since there was nothing, they could do for them, they just pumped me full of morphine. They sent me home that same night. Darlene got her first taste of being married to David. It was just a warmup for what would be expected of her if she was to live up to those wedding vows. Darlene says life with me was never dull!

The experiences I had from work with the hurricane and other disaster relief trips would lead Darlene and me to take a team of seven from our church to the hurricane Harvey area of Bay city to work yet again. We were able to cut down some trees, we tore down one destroyed home, making way for a new house to be built. We cleaned out another house that the roof had been torn off by the hurricane, destroying all the possessions of the older couple that live in it. It could not be evaluated by the insurance company until it was completely empty. Later we learned it had to be bulldozed. To be replaced with a travel trailer.

CHAPTER 24

A FINAL RODEO

*D*arlene and I had horses, one of which, I got to help deliver her colt. I had ridden most Sundays after Church. It was a bad day when our two donkeys, who liked to roam another people's property, especially our neighbor's hay field, got out and into that field. That just was not allowed, so one of our sons, Dalene and I went to get them out of the hay field.

We got a rope on one, who promptly took off running, the problem was that on the other end of that rope was our son, being pulled across the field, on his stomach, determined to stop the donkey, he would not turn loose of the rope. Somehow, we got him stopped enough for us to bulldog him long enough to put a halter on him so we could lead him back home.

Little did we know then that it would be my last rodeo. In the next days, my entire world would come crashing to an end.

CHAPTER 25

BACK AT HOME

*A*s I prepared for another good Sunday at the church, God had allowed me to open, for people without a relationship with God or people without a church to attend, due to broken relationships with God and His church. Some had been hurt by people in a church, some had never belonged to a church and others were recovering from other relationships or just life's troubles that can get us all at some time in our lives.

We were not a large church, maybe thirty or forty people on most weeks. After I gave Gods message, we would share a fried chicken dinner on each first Sunday of the month. I finally had answered Gods call on my life to Pastor His people. The church was making a difference in the lives of people. We gave love to whoever God brought to the church, telling the story of Jesus' love for us and His plan for our lives. Our people told others who would come. We were steadily growing. Life was fulfilling.

Now God had to lead me through the tragedy of a divorce, the suicide attempt, depression, then mission outreaches. A full circle back to Him and His original call of my life. To work with at least this group of hurting people, to guide them through Gods word, to find healing. Then to teach them how to tell others about what God had done in their lives. To lead them, not tell them to do it and run off to the next town, but to stay in one place. Doing what I had preached so often, lead. Our church had started with a very few and grown as God sent folks to us.

I met my good friend Richard Gonzales when God sent him to us in a most unusual way. Using tragedy to fulfill His good works. Richards, daughter's family, attending our church regularly, she had mentioned me to him at times but had no reaction from him. You see Richard had Pastored a church twenty-five years earlier. That group of people had mortally wounded him when he had to go through a divorce to save his children from an unhealthy situation at home. His church leaders told him he could no longer preach but could attend, sitting in the back of the building.

Richard did what most of us would, he told them he would not be back. Not able to understand how his fellow church members could reject him in his time of need. He turned angry then bitter toward all churches. Turning his back on Jesus too, he became a rough, tough, bike riding drunk and fighter. Oh, he took care of his children's needs by always having good jobs. But wanted nothing to do with preachers or churches.

One day God intervened in Richards life, God provided a way for Richard to want to redeem himself with Jesus.

As my new wife, Darlene and I were driving to town from our home in the country, we came over a small hill to see a man in a white pickup, pulling and trailer with a farm machine on it, he pulled out from a driveway on our side of the road right in front of us. We were driving the speed limit of seventy miles per hour when suddenly he was there, in front of us going very slowly.

As we were in a passing zone, Darlene swerved to our left to miss him and pass. However, just as we started pulling around the farmer, he turned suddenly to the left, pulling into another drive, across the road from where he had started.

We could either hit our brakes, which would cause us to skid, hitting him in his driver's door. Or we could speed up, trying to pass him on the shoulder of the road. There was only a split second to make the decision. I yelled to speed up, trying to get us around him, instead of possibly killing him if we crashed into his door at seventy miles an hour. Hoping to miss him and the terrible collision.

Darlene's driving and reaction timing were miraculous, as she shot around the front of the pickup, that had never stopped moving toward its destination. We were able to squeeze between the front grill of his truck on our right and a fence gate on the left.

Before we could celebrate the extremely narrow escape, we had to navigate out of the grassy ditch area we found ourselves in now, still traveling at least the seventy miles per hour, possibly even faster now. We had sped up, as we tried to race the other truck, to get around him before he closed the gap between himself and the gate he was trying to go through.

We had barely squeezed past his truck! Now Darlene tried to slow our vehicle by applying the brakes while pulling back on the paved road. That is when everything went wrong. Darlene lost control when we thought we had made it. The truck went sideways on the highway when we hit the pavement, we shot across the road into the ditch on the other side. Then we were suddenly going back the way we came from. We felt a significant drop as we went off a cement culvert nose first. The truck went over and around, through a fence and back on its wheels. The toolbox flew off as the back end of our vehicle came off the frame. Finally, we stopped,

DAVID GOAD

with both still in our seats. As we looked at each other, seeing if the other was alive and apparently not hurt badly.

The car behind us happened to be Richard and his family. After what Richard and his family had just seen of our truck disintegrating. They thought at the least, we would be terribly injured if not dead. They approached our mess cautiously, finding us both alive, and still in the cab, due to Darlene always insisting I wear a seat belt.

One of Richards granddaughters recognized us as her Pastor and wife. Richard came to my door expecting to at least see lots of blood. But God had protected Darlene and me that day, she always said a quiet prayer for protection before she left our home. Richard and I met that day. The ambulance took us away, only to find at the hospital, Darlene's only injury was a broken tailbone. My only damage was a knot on my head from hitting it on something in the wreck.

Afterward, Richard told his family that he thought God was telling him it was time to get his life right again. He started coming to our church as one of our most faithful. God even allowed Richard to preach again, filling in for me when I needed it most, after the Sunday that soon would change my life forever.

CHAPTER 26

THE STROKE

As I said, we had lunch together once a month in our church dining area. This was the first Sunday, it started like all other Sunday mornings, with our getting up at home. I spent time praying for God to use me, to give me the right words for the ones He brought that week. We then listened to Gospel music while we got ready for church. We got there early, as usual, to unlock and greet people as they came in.

I have never claimed to be a great speaker, but God has allowed me to show His love to those I have worked with, for me that meant loving on each person every week. Meeting them with a hug or handshake before church. Then talking with every one of them if possible, after church. To at least give a recognition that they were important to me. Especially at the church meals, when I had more time to get around to everyone.

This Sunday went just like it did each week. Barbara, our worship leader, lead the music and the opening prayer for us, then I would share the message, God had given me for that day.

About halfway through my message, that fateful morning, I felt something shift in my mind. It happened very quickly, like the blink of an eye. Almost unnoticeable, so fast that I really did not pay attention to it. However, after the service, Richard came up to me to say I did not need to comment on his story.

Slowly I started to realize, something had happened to me. I had shifted gears in my message, falling back on what was familiar, I guess. I do not know to this day if I told or said anything confidential about anyone. But it seems like I started pointing out people, instead of the message I had prepared.

At lunch, I did not mix as much as usual but went through the motions. Even helped carry food downstairs. To one lady's car, realizing later that my left arm was not carrying it very well. Instead, I rested the food tray on the handrail to slid it down, promising to make another trip down next. Instead, I sat on some steps, talking to my friend Richard and forgot all about it.

When we were leaving, our son and daughter in law, pulled up beside us to visit a minute. Our daughter in law said I did not look good that maybe I should go to the hospital. I said I was only tired; I would go home to rest instead.

By the next day, Darlene knew something was wrong with me. She took me to the Dr. who told me to take aspirin, but that if anything else happened, to take me to the Emergency Room of the hospital at once.

Tuesday morning, I was worse, she took me to the Emergency Room. Where they said I was having another stroke!

A stroke? Not me, I was strong. I was active on our small ranch, I handled the hay rolls, cut trees! I had just delivered our first filly. I had fought our errant donkey down to put a harness on him, leading him back home from our neighbor's pasture on Saturday? I could not be having a stroke??

However, I lost the use of my left side among other things that come with strokes. Like brain damage, losing cognitive skills, and much more. Suddenly as that, my life changed forever. I had to learn to walk again, to feed myself, I even had to learn how to spell my name, then how to write it again. I could not do the physical or mental things I had always taken to granted. Worst of all, I was not the man that Darlene had married, just a few years earlier.

Little did I know, but that stroke was only the start of the battles to come. As I was still recovering from the effects of the stroke, I started showing signs of heart trouble. Six months from the stroke, I back at the hospital to have a Catheter done. It is a procedure letting a doctor go in through an artery in my groin, to insert a tiny camera so he can see the arteries around the heart, to see any blockage a person might have in those arteries, feeding blood to the heart.

The four arteries feeding my heart were all blocked, some

as much as ninety percent. They needed emergency open-heart surgery for a quadruple bypass. I woke up much later to find I had my chest cracked open. I am sure they must have played handball with my heart, while they had it out, then stuck it back and stapled me back together. Whatever they had done hurt terribly to breathe. I had a tube down my throat another one coming out of my side. I took three transfusions of blood because I bled so badly.

Darlene and a Pastor friend came into my room in intensive care to say goodnight, just as my eyes rolled up in my head. A code 99, for emergency heart failure, went out causing lots of nurses to show up in my room all at once. My pulse dropped to thirty-two beats per minute.

I still needed one of those three transfusions. Still bleeding inside, my liver was bleeding, from those years of heavy drinking, I had developed sclerosis causing a third of my liver to die.

The medical team rushed my wife out while they got my pulse back up. God had intervened again in my life; He just was not done with me yet.

At some time during this, I had an experience that I will never forget! I saw my Mother and Grandmother standing on the far side of a great opening, both were there as young women, both were watching what was happening to me. With a peaceful but watchful look on their faces, quietly they watched over me. Just to the right of them, and a little behind was a figure, I could only see the shape. But I had the impression that it was enormous in width and height. Its color was like a very brilliant white-gold color, it was so radiant, that I only could see its magnificence. I had the impression that is was an Angel.

The whole scene created in me a feeling of inner peace that I have never felt before or since, that all was going to be right. Then all three gone.

I do not claim to understand what happened or how I saw them, I only know that the image burned into my memory, so that it can never be forgotten.

About six weeks later, as I was home, beginning to heal from the surgery, I awoke early one morning with a horrible weight on my chest. I thought it must be indigestion, but the pressure got worse instead of better. Waking Darlene, telling her that it felt like a freight train was sitting on my chest.

It felt like I was having a heart attack, but we could not believe that could happen, I was just getting over the open-heart surgery. To fix my heart with assurance, I should be good for another twenty to thirty years now.

Darlene called the Emergency Room anyway, the nurse listened to her description of what I felt like, she told us it did not matter about the surgery, I could still have and was having a heart attack. Hang up and call the ambulance at once.

It turned out the bypass had failed. All my arteries had closed back up. After another attack while in the hospital, they took me back to install seven stints, to keep the arteries open.

In just a few months, I had been through a stroke, open-heart surgery, heart attacks, and stints, all while still Pastoring our church. Jesus had to walk with and carry me a lot during that time, but the church was patient. After all, it was the prayers of very many friends appealing to God, that had saved my life, multiple times.

God allowed me to Pastor five more years, making it ten years total. God had appointed this most unlikely man, to lead those people He had entrusted to me, teaching them to grow in the love of Jesus, to love each other and the unlovable. To forgive hurts, rejoin families long since separated. Some left drug and alcohol addictions behind, and many met Jesus for the very first time.

To have Black, White and Hispanic all worshipping and loving together. Learning to trust each other, to work together, making this world a little better place. Starting in our own neighborhood, then spreading to other parts of our society.

We believed and taught that Jesus is the only Son of God the Father, who sent His only Son Jesus, to live and to die among us as a man.

That Jesus gave His life for our sin or wrongs, becoming the greatest sacrifice for all time, so you and I would never again have to offer sacrifices for ourselves, but only believe in Jesus and ask His forgiveness for our wrongs,

So that by truly repenting or turning our back on those wrongs, we might be saved from the eternal consequences of those sins.

While we may still have consequences in our lives here in this world. We are promised eternal life with Jesus in Heaven, free of any consequences forever. No more sickness of any kind, no more sorrow of any kind. Only joy and love forever.

The experiences I had with hurricane disaster relief would lead Darlene and me to take a team of seven to the hurricane Harvey area of Bay city to work yet again. We were able to cut down some trees, we tore down one almost destroyed home, making way for a new house to be built. We cleaned out another house that the roof had been torn off by the hurricane, destroying all the possessions of the older couple living there. It could not be evaluated by the insurance company until it was completely empty. Later we learned it had to be bulldozed. To be replaced with a travel trailer.

I have recently retired from Pastoring at age seventy. God sent us a great replacement Pastor. I had to give up our horses and donkeys while I was so sick. We thought I would never be able to ride again. As the truck was on its way to our home to pick up the horses, I decided to take one more ride on my favorite. I was afraid to get my saddle and tack; I thought my wife would not allow me to make this ride.

So, I hid behind the barn, made a halter out of hay bale cords. I found that I could no longer just get on my horse without help. Looking around, I saw a six-foot ladder. The perfect way to climb up on 'Mo' my horse. He stood perfectly still for me, I stood the ladder up next to him, climbed up the ladder and swung my left leg over his bare back. Then I started to settle on his back for that last ride.

I was so satisfied with myself for figuring out how to do this, that I got a little excited and careless. So just as I was settling down, I let go of the ladder with my right leg. The ladder shifted just enough so that it hit my horse in his flank. I saw him tense his back but could do nothing to stop what happened next.

'Mo' shot out from under me like a racehorse. I hung in the air for a moment, then straight down to land flat, except for my left wrist. I felt it break, but I also got a mouthful of dried horse manure. I came off the ground spitting out the manure, thinking, yuck! This is what we have been feeding these guys?

My wrist started telling me it was broken, just as the truck was pulling into our driveway. Pulling my arm up and shirt sleeve down, I covered up my boo-boo until the horses had been loaded, I said my tearful goodbyes to my beloved horses, and they drove away.

Going into the house I told Darlene I was going to lay down a bit, but my wrist kept throbbing and began swelling up. Finally, I said to Darlene about that I thought my wrist broken. Now I had to explain how it had gotten broken. Expecting a real chewing out, I got near hysterical laughing. She said she would have helped me take the last ride if I had told her I wanted to. But such is the logic of a stroke survivor. Talk about adding insult to injury, as she took me to the Emergency Room for my broken wrist, she called everyone she could think of, telling them about my fiasco.

With an Emergency Room full of hurting and sick people, laughter is not really what they want to hear. But all we could do was laugh, at my expense, naturally.

The End

AUTHORS BIOGRAPHY

*D*avid has lived the life he talks about. His journey from having been molested as a young boy, by a trusted family friend, being introduced to alcohol with the resulting slide downhill from a successful salesman until the final unemployed crash and jail time. The warning of the next arrest ending in prison time. David's long struggle back to sanity and finally how Jesus came into his life to *Transform* it forever.

How God took him from four divorces and five arrests, with time in a Texas jail, to his opportunities to serve Jesus with the Jesus Video Project of America, work in Washington DC, his visit to the Whitehouse and Congress, even mailing of 10,000 Jesus videos to every senator or house of representative and their key assistant.

The return to Texas, with the tests of faith, through the last arrest, divorce and significant health issues including strokes, heart failure, heart attacks, and seizures. All to destroy what God wanted to do through one man with one plan. To tell as many people about the saving Love of Jesus as possible, before being called home to eternal peace with God. Not to be defeated by Satan, God allowed David to be spared repeatedly.

In time he was given a new, Godly wife, to share ministry and to care for him through two potentially fatal car wrecks and all the health issue. Darlene nursed him back to life in both, physical and emotional health. Always encouraging David with her love and spiritual strength. Praying over him when he had seizures, ever able to calm his mind and spirit, restoring in him the fighting will to overcome.

As the rebirth of 'American Renewal movement' grew to a church, David Pastored with Darlene's faithful help, for 10 years before David retired at age 71. Handing the church Pastorate to a dear friend and his wife. However, God is still blessing. David has finally told his story of God's transformation from a wasted life to a powerful witness of God's Grace and love waiting for all of us. By authoring this book, by using internet blogging, social media, and public speaking, David continues reaching the lost for Christ.

The experiences David shares with us, of David and friends introduced along the way, like Bill who showed him the way back to Jesus, Bob, who first believed in him. Bob introduced David to the Jesus video project. Steve, who shares his own testimony of being crushed alive in a pile of trash in the dump, and Mario, who has become a spiritual warrior in his own life, as well as a friend for life.

David has a unique ability to share with the reader the exciting, and sometimes tragic story of how a life can be Transformed, from beyond hope, to victory through Jesus,

David lives in West Texas, with his wife Darlene and their two dogs. They have four adult children, nine grandchildren, and one great-granddaughter.

This book is also dedicated to Jesus Christ, with whom I would never have experienced the most exciting part of my life. It is also dedicated to my Mother (Mary Lou), and grandmother, (Ruby Earl), who believed in me and prayed me into the Heaven I will know when this worldly journey is over. To those who have been with me on the journey. Especially my wife Darlene, who with her constant prayers, love and attention, nursed me back to health of body, mind, soul.

My family. Brothers Jerry and Jim, Sister Lynda. Also, our kids Dave, Shannon, Shaina, Shane and all the grandkids, nephews, nieces and friends who have believed in this project and encouraged me throughout the time it has taken to write it. Thanks to each of you and God Bless!

Without the two people who helped edit this book, it would not have been published. Thank you, Shawna, who translated my voice recordings into words, even when they did not make sense.

And my friend Amy who had spent hours encouraging me when I thought I could not finish. When my mind would not work well enough, you helped keep me on track and moving forward with gentle suggestions. You took my mess of misspelled words and sentences turned them into a readable form. I cannot thank you enough Amy and Alton who proofread it for us!

Printed in the United States
By Bookmasters